The
Young
Adult
Generation

The
Young
Adult
Generation

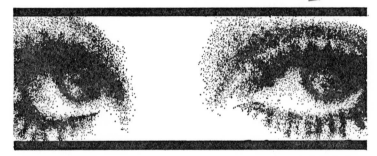

A Perspective on the Future

Allen J. Moore

Nashville—ABINGDON PRESS—New York

THE YOUNG ADULT GENERATION

Copyright © 1969 by Abingdon Press

Standard Book Number: 687-46766-7

Library of Congress Catalog Card Number: 69-18443

SET UP, PRINTED, AND BOUND BY THE
PARTHENON   PRESS,   AT   NASHVILLE,
TENNESSEE, UNITED STATES OF AMERICA

Preface

It is my belief that empirical research does not support the popular notion that there is a massive generation gap in our society. Instead, it is my thesis that what we have with the present young adults is what can be described as a "post-modern generation." They are the first generation to have modern parents who broke the shackles of tradition and gave birth to social, moral, and religious revolutions. This present young adult generation has only continued to feed the change which has been going on in our society for several decades.

This position may be viewed by some as conservative. I actually see it as being far more radical than the generation-gap theory that has helped to create the myth that these new young adults are of some special breed. My findings have led me to conclude that something far more profound is going on in our culture. Young adults do not establish revolutions as much as they reflect the deep and far-reaching changes which are already taking place in society. A study of the new young adult generation is significant because it gives us a clue as to where we are going as a society of people.

It is my conclusion that three things can be learned from young adults. The first is that they reflect the times in which we live. The second is that they are a forward wave of society and a preview of a new age of radical humanism. And the third is, young adults provide a basic perspective on the future and a clue of things to come.

There have been many books written on the new generation of youth and young adults. But most of these works have been impressionistic and have served only to establish the myth that young adults are the new messiahs of our age. I believe that empirical research does not support many of the popular assumptions which have been written or spoken about this new generation. As a result, my conclusions do not glorify young adults or acknowledge a basic disjunction between them and the rest of society. I have turned to empirical research and have tried to "tell it like it is."

The nature of the book is interpretative research. I have taken seriously the available research data insofar as it was available to me. But like Edgar Friedenberg, I have not limited my commentary just to hard data. I have not hesitated to use clinical observations or findings from my own participation with young adults and to make interpretations of the evidence. Basically I write as a theologian who is attempting to take seriously social and psychological data in order to know what is going on and to be able to make theological judgments upon contemporary man and

6

his culture. In other words, as a theologian I am concerned with what young adults are saying to us about our age. It is my belief that in the new young adult generation we can find some insight as to what it means to come of age and to achieve a new maturity. *In short, young adults point to the potentialities of our human future as well as to some of the terrible pitfalls.*

No one writes a book without the aid of others. The National Young Adult Project provided assistance in the formulation of the book and provided documents and research data. The Rev. Earl R. Willford, staff member of the project, read the manuscript in full and made valuable comments. The manuscript was also read by Dr. Glen O. Martin of the Department of Campus Ministry of the General Board of Education of The United Methodist Church. Some of the most valuable assistance came from David Sharrard, my research assistant here at the School of Theology. He has not only helped in the gathering of research material, but has read the manuscript and has made some important corrections to my argument. He also prepared the index. Mrs. Paul McReynolds, my able and generous secretary, has typed the manuscript. As is customary for authors to say, the book is finally my responsibility.

My wife Jean and our daughters, Glenda, Joyce, and Nan, have encouraged me in the writing and have protected my time to insure the completion of the book. They have all kept alert to the young adult field, and each in her own way has insured her point of view from time to time.

Dr. Ross Snyder of Chicago Theological Seminary alerted me a decade ago to the importance of the young adult situation. At that time I was serving as National Director of Young Adult Work for The Methodist Church, and Dr. Snyder assisted me in a consultation on young adults when the larger society had not yet become sensitive to the bulging young adult population. He has pioneered in the study of youth and young adults and has made the greatest contribution to my thinking. I have long forgotten what belongs to him and what is my own thinking. To my mind, he is one of the most creative theologians of our time and has served me as a spiritual and intellectual father. It is to Prof. Snyder that I dedicate this work.

ALLEN J. MOORE

Contents

9

1

The New Generation

Young adulthood is a cultural phenomenon as well as a particular time in life. The generalization that young people have always had to pass through the late teens and twenties on their way to adult maturity is of course true. But it is equally true that what we have come to know as the "new young adult generation" is a distinctive feature of our times. Never in history has a society had so many persons coming to maturity at the same time and seldom has a youth culture been so dominant in its influence. Our way of life, our values, our forms of work and leisure, our style of dress, and even our houses and automobiles have been influenced greatly by the "youthful look."

Coming of age is both a psychosocial process and a cultural happening. As Erik H. Erikson has demonstrated in his remarkable study of the young adult years of Martin Luther, the genetic and psychological crises of an age stage are inherent in human nature and are always present. It is the way these characteristic crises arise to ascendancy, become manifest, and are resolved that marks the distinctiveness of a generation.[1] A new generation always comes of age in relation to a particular cultural setting that defines and influences the way persons are to become adults. In the maturing process the culture is in turn influenced and sometimes greatly altered.

The present young adult generation cannot lightly be dismissed as another generation of rebellious youth. Probably never before in history has a new generation been so dominant in reflecting and shaping the massive changes that are now taking place at all levels of human life. Social revolutions have given rise to a new kind of generation that has in turn given birth to a revolution of its own. To say that we have always had young adults may only lead us to miss altogether the significance of this age group.

Michael Harrington begins his book *The Accidental Century* with these words: "In the twentieth century, something enormous is being born. And something enormous is dying." [2] Culturally speaking, the new young adult generation is symbolic of the new era that is taking shape in our society.

A "Coming-of-Age" Generation

It can be argued, I believe, that the contemporary young adult generation is actually the manifestation of what Dietrich Bonhoeffer described as the "world coming of age." Young adults are not only going through a personal

---

[1] *Young Man Luther* (New York: W. W. Norton, 1958).

[2] (New York: The Macmillan Co., 1965), p. 13.

12

transition from adolescence to adulthood, but are also a part of a cultural transition in which mankind is in the process of growing up.

While in a Gestapo concentration camp as a political prisoner, Bonhoeffer wrote his famous *Letters and Papers from Prison*.[3] This book, along with other of his writings, has provided a basis for a social theology of our times.[4] His popularity among the less conventional types of young adults is largely due to the secular interpretation which he provided for a world that these young adults are attempting to take seriously. Bonhoeffer has been one of the idols of the young activists who see his civil resistance to the policies of Hitler as an ethical rationale for secular action and a basis for civil opposition to the injustices of race, poverty, and war.

In a brief but amazing way Bonhoeffer was able to articulate nearly twenty-five years ago the cultural transition that has come to a climax in the midst of the present generation of young adults. He foresaw the decline of religion in the affairs of men and the decadence of the institutional church. Humanity would outgrow supernaturalism and would no longer have an adolescent-type dependency upon the natural forces which had in the past so controlled the destiny of men. Mankind was growing up, coming of age, and becoming adult. The world was reaching adulthood and in the process was achieving a new maturity, a new independence, and a new freedom. Bonhoeffer believed that God was being edged out of the world

[3] (New York: The Macmillan Co., 1953).
[4] Especially his *Ethics*, ed. Eberhard Bethge (New York: The Macmillan Co., 1955).

and would no longer be needed by men as a working hypothesis or as a solver of human problems. The new autonomy of man would make it possible for man to answer his own questions and meet his own needs without resorting to divine help.

In short, Bonhoeffer offered the myth of a post-religious man, oriented not to other worlds but to a secular existence in the present world of men. He saw increasingly that temporal matters would supersede religious matters and that the human quality of life would outdate religious piety and asceticism. What was required of men was to embrace fully the world, to enter completely into the affairs of men, and to be fully human.

The new generation of young adults seems to be to a large extent a prototype of Bonhoeffer's myth of a world coming of age. The young adults reflect the growing autonomy of human life and man's increasing confidence in his ability to handle his own affairs without the aid of religion. This is evidenced by the conclusions of Emmanuel G. Mesthene, executive director of the Harvard University Program on Technology and Society. He believes that we are witnessing what he calls "a widespread recovery of nerve." What Mesthene means is that man is no longer turning to God for understanding or to secure help to do those things which he knows he can do himself. He writes:

> I think things are changing. I doubt that there are many men today who would question that life will be produced in the laboratory, that psychologists and their personality drugs will soon reveal what really makes men tick, that scientific prediction is a far more promising guide to the future than divination, and

14

that the heavens cannot long remain mysterious in the
face of our ability to hit the moon today and the stars
tomorrow.[5]

Increasingly, among young adults who have grown up
under the influence of science and technology, there is
evidenced a growing confidence in man's ability to solve his
own problems, an enlarged faith in a universe which holds
no secrets, and a belief in the essential intelligibility of the
moral. The moral temper of the young adult is that of a
world coming of age.

A Time of Change

Young adulthood is a time of change. In actuality the
new age that young adults seem to depict has been emerging for centuries. History will indicate that the decline of
religion—the movement toward secularity and an age of
accelerated change—has been taking place ever since the
thirteenth or fourteenth centuries. The stage for an adult
world has been set ever since the rise of modern times, the
development of the scientific method, and the discovery of
the human sciences.

World War II is generally considered as the climactic
turning point in history at which the death of the old order
became apparent and the birth of a new order became
inevitable. Granted there are semblances of the old order
still remaining, and at times they make noises as if death
were yet a long way off. But the truth of the matter is that

[5] "Learning to Live with Science," *Saturday Review*, July 17, 1965,
p. 14.

the events of the 1940's set history on a new course, and there has been little evidence that society would turn back, even if it could. Actually, human history has reached the point of no return. The forces of change have already pushed us into the twenty-first century, and to a large extent we are living in what Hans Hoekendijk described as "the day after tomorrow."

It was during the mid-1940's that the present young adult generation started to come into being, in what has come to be known as the population explosion or the "baby boom." The parents of this generation were returning servicemen and war brides who themselves composed the first identifiable subculture of young adults. These young parents migrated to the cities in large numbers in a search for freedom. Breaking the shackles of tradition, they stood on the threshold of a future that was to be largely uncharted. In the midst of unprecedented prosperity, educational opportunities, and technological developments, children of these postwar years moved toward adulthood. Within their lifetimes they have experienced the far-reaching consequences of revolutions in technology, communications, urbanization, education, relations between the sexes, and even in religious belief and morality. They have come of age under the influence of television, jet air travel, computers and automation, new mathematics, space exploration, cold wars, ideological struggles, and massive advancements in the physical and psychological sciences, medicine, and pharmacy. The futuristic visions of science fiction have become a reality for most young adults.

Young people tend to be precise indicators of what is going on within a society. Gibson Winter sees young adulthood as a giant prism that reflects what is happening to society, revealing the best and worst features of the times.

In young adults can be seen the extent to which society is changing as well as the problems and the opportunities inherent in such change. The pitfalls of the young generation are sometimes missed in the present tendency to overglamorize youth. It is a hopeful age group that manifests the best of the times. But it is also a terribly complex age group that is caught up in some of the greatest problems in human history. Cut loose from traditional mooring, young adults, because of the power that comes from sheer numbers, have the opportunity to shape a new future for society. But they are equally in danger of becoming self-seeking and, under the guise of freedom, leading society into a new anarchy.

Fortunately, the young adult influence upon society has been largely constructive. It has awakened us to the massive problems of poverty, unemployment, education, war, human brutality, racism, pollution, overpopulation, amorality, depersonalization, and the loss of human meaning. They have demonstrated against the apathy of a society that is capable of change but is more inclined to coast in the security of the past. In fact, one of the reasons that this generation has become such a threat to the adult society is that it has exposed the myth that improving traditional institutions, such as churches, schools, law enforcement, and economic affluence will not in itself eliminate the core problems of humanity. They will be resolved only as society comes to new ways of viewing mankind and to a new understanding of the nature of human interdependency. The old social structures were to a large extent formulated

17

to serve the individualistic man who got ahead on his own initiative and who provided paternalistic care for those who were not as fortunate as he. New social structures are required today that will acknowledge the common humanity shared by all men and reflect the implosion that brings all men into a closer relationship. The welfare of any one man today depends upon the universal welfare of all men.

So far in our society the rapidity of social change has heightened the differences between the advantaged and the disadvantaged and widened the gap between the haves and have-nots. Social advancement has tended to enrich and strengthen the advantages already enjoyed by the middle and upper classes and to further reinforce the lack of opportunity and the repression experienced by the poor whites and colored minorities.

Nowhere is social alienation more clearly seen than in the young adult age group. There are literally thousands of young men and women in our nation who are trapped by the same forces that have produced the new age and have benefited the majority. Michael Harrington has included them in his description of the "new poor," the people who are more entrenched in poverty because of the new technology and whose desire to escape has been heightened by the visions of a better life supplied by television.[6] The result has been a growing anger and open violence on the part of these dispossessed young people.

The unwillingness of the established adult community to respond to these young adults has become one of the most

[6] *The Other American* (New York: The Macmillan Co., 1962), especially chap. I.

18

serious indictments upon our way of life. Inequalities in education, employment, housing, cultural enrichment, and health services are only a few of the ways through which society is limiting the humanity of its new generation.

Even the advantaged young adult has come to a growing sensitivity to the plight of at least one third of his age group. There is evidence that a basic search is being made by this generation in an effort to find those values and goals which will make for a more human life. A shift in basic commitment on the part of many young adults is exemplified by the shift in vocational goals toward those careers concerned with human services. A study of Harvard students, made in 1956, revealed that a majority desired to go into business or work for big corporations. But by 1966 more Harvard seniors entered the Peace Corps than took up careers in business.

Young adults provide an interesting contrast of a society that has never had it so good while at the same time never having it so bad. As Paul Goodman points out, it is difficult, if not impossible, to achieve adulthood if your immediate environment does not include goals, experiences, and opportunities to make growing up worthwhile.[7] The society of the 1950's, based upon bland conformity, privatism, and middle-class values of sociality was not ready for the sudden impact of the technological age. Increasingly it is apparent: The established society just is not prepared to integrate a new generation that it has helped to nurture and awaken to the possibilities of the changing times.

[7] *Growing Up Absurd* (New York: Random House, 1960), pp. 11 ff.

Changing Urban World

Urban society is one of the major components of the young adult world. The young adult has grown up in the midst of rapid urbanization. By urbanization we mean those sociological processes by which the environment and natural resources are transformed into what Cox calls "settings for human life." The more intensive the transformation, the more urban the society becomes. The extent to which urbanization has spread is illustrated by the fact that more than 3,000 acres per day are converted to urban settings. New metropolises emerge out of the conversion of raw or agricultural land into streets and freeways, living tracts, business and industrial districts, and recreational areas. With the rise of giant cities extending for hundreds of miles, it has been necessary for more and more land to be converted into green belts and wilderness parks for use by urban dwellers.

Urban society is also the result of increasing numbers of persons living within limited land space. As the density of population increases, urbanization results. Today more than four fifths of the nation's population live in metropolitan areas. This increase has been rapidly occurring since the close of World War II, and all projections indicate that it will continue for some time. Since 1950, the population in the 212 metropolitan areas increased by more than 10 percent—an increase 2½ times greater than in nonmetropolitan areas. The rate of growth has been increasing most in the suburbs, although the nonwhite population has continued to climb rapidly in the central cities.

Urbanization is a worldwide phenomenon due largely

to an increasing population and a changing economy. For instance, urbanization is going forward at a much more rapid rate than ever before in Latin America, Africa, and Asia because of increases in natural birth and because of in-migration, primarily of young adults. Much of the increase in the central cities in this country has been caused also by the in-migration of young adults along with racial minorities. It is interesting to observe that this in-migration of the young has become so extensive in some countries— such as Russia and the African nations—that permission of the government is now required before a person can move to the city.

The changing economy has contributed to urban growth. The mechanization of agriculture has reduced the need for manpower on the farm, and the increased aggregation of people in the cities has increased the need for personal service. Today less than 10 percent of the population is required for food production, and this very shortly will go down to 5 percent. On the other hand, the need for persons in the personal service occupations—mechanics, repairmen, barber and beauty shop operators, travel agents, those connected with leisure-time occupations, etc.—has multiplied many times. Service occupations are primarily urban based and are one of the reasons why young adults go to the city.

Educational opportunities as well as the possibility for employment have also accounted for part of the urban growth. Unfortunately, many go to the city without training or without either the motivation or opportunity to attend urban schools and therefore do not qualify for the increasing specialization of human work.

The close proximity of people living in urban society is changing the character of human life. Many urban critics glamorize the character of life in pre-urban America and argue that the loss of primary relationships is leading to the gross depersonalization of human life. This has led some institutions, such as the church, to artificially create primary relationships for their adherents. But this is not only contrary to the functional nature of urban society, but is also a negation of what urban man needs and wants. As Harvey Cox has argued, the city not only requires but affords anonymity.[8] Anonymity is a requirement for maintaining a more human life. In urban society there is a clear distinction between public and private life. There is an advantage in being able to withdraw from public affairs into a private retreat in order to reflect, relax, or just let oneself go. In contrast to rural society in which all of life was public, urban society permits opportunities for people to take off their masks and be authentically free of pretension.

In a real sense a new kind of human personalism seems to be emerging in urban society. Some call it professional friendliness because it is often cultivated through training or as a part of a company's policy. The airline stewardess is trained to be personable and attentive. And yet there is more to it than that. Young adults belong to a generation that is basically "up on people." Urban man, especially the young urban dweller who does not have to contend with casting off old rural mores, is more open to human life in all of its varieties. There is, on one hand, a more ready

---

[8] *The Secular City* (New York: The Macmillan Co., 1965), pp. 39 ff.

22

acceptance of that which is different and, on the other hand, a greater sense of universality in the city. It is this polarity that marks urban life.

The small-town friendliness that we sometimes glorify was actually limited to the ingroup. The outsider was always under suspicion, and close relationships were either avoided all together or kept very formal. In contrast, urban relations tend to be instant, personal, often functional, and also often very meaningful. The city provides new avenues for involvement as well as occasions to withdraw from people altogether.

The urbanity of young adult culture is a sociological fact. The young adult generation has both contributed to the rise of urban culture and been shaped by it. Approximately 75 to 80 percent of this young adult generation now lives in urban areas.

It can be argued that society did not have a period in life known as young adulthood until urbanization required it. A transitional age group between youth and adulthood is seldom found in primitive societies and is not needed in most rural social structures. In fact, in rural America the youth years were extended to include the twenties, and adulthood was simply marked by marriage and the taking of one's place on the farm or in the family trade. The brevity of the transition did not eliminate all of the problems, but the closeness of the family and the primary groups of the community tended to ease the pain and to provide models and direction for the young man or woman taking his or her place in adult society.

Urbanization increases the complexity of human life and results in increased specificity of age groupings. In fact,

Erik Erikson seems to feel that there will be further specificity of age groupings, especially in the youth and young adult years. He sees emerging "young adult specialists," older young adults who will assume responsibility for the younger young adults. He writes that their power, "in many ways, will replace the sanction of tradition or, indeed, of parents." [9] Jencks sees this already taking place on the university campus[10] and I believe there is evidence of young adult specificity in the hippie movement and in young adult living communities such as the luxury apartments. It is certainly apparent that graduate students have become the guides and leaders of the undergraduates, legitimatizing the undergraduates' struggles toward adulthood and providing examples of discontent and rebellion and models of new styles of life. Such "specialists" may be required in order for youth to successfully grow up in a time of rapid change, especially when all indications are that society will continue to be in a state of high flux and that change will accelerate in the future.

Young people of the present generation are coming of age in a historical period that is experiencing the breakdown of traditional communities, the crumbling of traditions and stated values, the diversification of adult models, the changing function of the family, and the increasing mobility of the population. All these have increased the difficulties of moving from a youth world of dependency to an adult world of interdependency. Today most of the post-childhood years are spent outside the context of the family, with the young

[9] "Memorandum on Youth," *Daedalus,* Summer, 1967, p. 868.
[10] Christopher Jencks and David Riesman, "The War Between the Generations," *Teachers College Record,* October, 1967, pp. 10 f.

adult years being spent largely in a highly transitory environment almost void of significant adult relations.[11] Upon graduation or dropping out of high school, young people are cast adrift from stable moorings into an almost all-youth culture, to work out for themselves adult relationships and responsibilities. As others have argued, a distinctive mark of urban society is the large number of youth and young adults who are able to come together in institutions that will separate them from the rest of society. Examples of this are urban universities with thirty thousand young adults enrolled or living communities with two or three hundred residents, all under thirty years of age. This separation from society has led to what has been described as a dominant young adult subculture; young adults, involved in large numbers in such close relationships, are able to reinforce one another in the development of new social traits, attitudes, and styles of life.

In many ways urban society represents a series of contradictions in regard to young adults. On one hand, they are told to hurry up and grow up. But, on the other hand, society has a decreasing need for more new adults. The growing tension between the generations is related in part to the inability of adults to integrate in meaningful ways the host of young men and women who are reaching adulthood. Presently, the one institution in society that requires young adults is the military. As it has always been, young adults

[11] An example of this was the main complaint of the students in the recent rebellions on university campuses. The undergraduates are assigned primarily to teaching assistants and young instructors, with few opportunities to be with mature adults in meaningful ways. Those of us who have moved in and out of the hippie community found a hunger there for adult relationships.

25

are expected to fight the wars which adults have made. But young adults today are providing an exception to this traditional adult assumption. Possibly for the first time in any large number, young adults are resisting military service and are demanding that the adult establishment put an end to military conflict as a means of resolving political problems. This is not because this generation of young men are any less brave or patriotic; rather it reflects the growing belief that modern warfare is immoral and inhuman.

In spite of the multitude of new occupations young adults entering the labor force are displacing large numbers of older workers. This is especially true in unskilled and non-technical fields. The complexity of modern urban society and the need to regulate entrance into the labor force has resulted in the extension of educational expectation for almost every occupation and profession. This results not only in oversocialization (gaining more social skills than are actually needed), but also in increased social and economic dependency of the young upon adults. Such dependency increases the tensions between generations and often leads to outbreaks of hostility. Goodman, Friedenberg, and others have well substantiated that the extension of educational requirements has not necessarily resulted in a more meaningful education or a sense of worthwhileness on the part of the young.[12]

---

[12] Paul Goodman, "The University's Role in Contemporary Society," *Problems of Authority and Identity in the University*, ed. William A. Overholt, pp. 1 ff. This is the Report of the Twentieth Annual Conference, National Association of College and University Chaplains and Directors of Religious Life, April 3-6, 1967, at Boston University. See also Edgar Z. Friedenberg, *The Vanishing Adolescent* (Boston: Beacon Press, 1959).

All the forces of the new age are contributing to an earlier maturity of young people, while social structures tend to maintain and even extend the years of dependency upon adults. Such contradictions have led Bruno Bettelheim to suggest that young adults have actually become the older generation's greatest economic liability.[13] As a result, the major problem for urban society today may not be young adults so much as adults. There is growing evidence that the urban struggle is for a place in the work force and in the power structure. It is natural for most adults to be threatened by the rise of a large population of young people who are in most instances better educated, more urbane and sophisticated, and more eager to establish themselves in positions of influence. As long as society has room for additional adults and has a need to make replacements in the established society, the transitional process from one generation to another is fairly smooth. But let large numbers of youth come on the scene and begin to crowd out adults, and conflict between the generations becomes inevitable.[14]

The New Technology

The rapid development of the new technology has also served to shape the character of the new young adult generation. As Marshall McLuhan has pointed out, we are passing from the old mechanical age to the new electrical age. Every aspect of our personal and social life is being reshaped by the impact of the new electrical media. It is not only unify-

[13] "The Problem of Generations," *Daedalus,* Winter, 1962, p. 78.
[14] For a technical discussion of this point see Samuel N. Eisenstadt, *From Generation to Generation* (New York: The Free Press, 1956), particularly chap. I.

ing life, but is also drawing persons into a new level of human involvement. The youth of our society are particularly influenced by the new technology. Young adult life has been, according to McLuhan, "electrified," and young adults live mythically, with depth, and with a greater involvement in the total scope of human affairs.[15] This is dramatically exemplified by the adjectives we use to describe young adults: the "cool" generation, the "now" generation, the "open" generation, and the "turned-on" generation are all images charged with electrical connotations.

The new technological age came into being in August, 1945, with the explosion of the atom bomb and the experience of its massive destructive power. This generation of young adults has never been far from the potential destruction of the whole human race. They are the first generation to grow up entirely under the influence of atomic energy, electronics, automation, and rocket power. Leaving behind the pessimism characteristic of the fifties, they have come to understand increasingly that the technology that provides the power of mass destruction also offers the potentiality for a more human life for all races and nations of people. Technology has ushered into being an era in which the young people of the world are deeply involved in finding peaceful solutions to the conflicts of men. The peace movement is largely related to the developments in technology which have made the old morality inadequate in the face of new methods of human destruction. At the same time, modern communications has opened the doors of the world, and young people from all nations have lifted their voices

[15] Marshall McLuhan and Quentin Fiore, *The Medium Is the Massage* (New York: Bantam Books, 1967), pp. 8-9.

in criticism of the old order. The new technology has contributed to the shrinking of the universe and has united the young adults of the world in a common search for a new order.

John Dewey, thirty years ago, foresaw the coming of the age of technology and declared that it would become basically a human problem. His fear was that man's social consciousness would not keep pace with his discoveries in the realm of science. In many respects he was correct in his prediction. The rising tide of protest on the part of the young has been partly due to society's lack of sensitivity to the growing imbalance between man's scientific capabilities and his ethical formulations. The new technology, rather than creating the nightmare of a "brave new world," has led man to an increasing sensitivity to his ethical responsibilities, and this is nowhere more evident than among the young.

In his book *The Meaning of the 20th Century*, Kenneth E. Boulding describes what he has called the great transition: the movement from a civilized to a post-civilized society.[16] What he means is that we have been in the process for sometime of moving from a work-oriented, legalistic, stable society to a mass-media, cybernetic, change-oriented society. As William Hamilton points out, "Boulding's book describes the mood of those who are saying *yes* to the radical changes in our society, *yes* to technology, *yes* to all the new and even threatening ways that man is finding to handle the world in which he lives." [17]

[16] (New York: Harper & Row, 1964), pp. 1-26.
[17] *Radical Theology and the Death of God* (Indianapolis: Bobbs-Merrill, 1966), p. 160.

The young adult mood is basically optimistic. By optimistic I mean reflecting a confidence in the future of humanity and a belief that life is good. Probably nowhere in our society has the young adult culture been as dominant as in our contemporary music. True, much of this music centers upon protest and subtle hostility toward adult institutions. But much of it also represents celebration, the affirmation of love, personal aliveness, and the worth of human life. Young adults are sometimes "cool"; that is, they are caught up in the modern scene, moving with the times, and able to respond without coming apart in the contingencies of an ever-changing situation.

It is more than science fiction to suggest that the new technology has already pushed us into the twenty-first century and the young adult represents a vision of the new man. Urbanization and technology combine to create a new kind of city that I have called "electropolis." As Harvey Cox has pointed out, "the world is becoming one huge interdependent city." [18] This is not to suggest that there is not ambiguity in the future. The problems are immense, and human suffering is evident everywhere. But because we are so aware and sensitive to what is taking place all around us, there is the hope that the new generation will lead the whole of society toward creating a new civilization.

The new environment that is arising from technology and cybernetics makes isolation almost impossible. The industrial city with its isolated suburbs is already beginning to decline. Man can no longer escape from the issues of the new society by re-creating on the fringes of the city a pastoral

[18] *On Not Leaving It to the Snake* (New York: The Macmillan Co., 1967), p. 102.

environment. Television and radio break that isolation and bring the issues of the world into his home. This is most potently exemplified in the inability of the white man to escape any longer the hostility and hatred which is rising up in the black man. No one can be man nowadays unless everyone is permitted to be.

The new environment can most accurately be described as an electric, cybernetic, dynamic social system. What this suggests is that we no longer live in just one city or even a regional metropolis. Our home is now the universe—a global city in which the whole of humanity is linked together in one environmental communicative system of exchange. McLuhan has characterized this development as the emergence of a new tribal society—a way of life based upon human familiarity, intimacy, and personal involvement. Even now most young adults are more at home in distant places than in their immediate neighborhoods. Life is no longer determined by the day-by-day existence in a closed society, but by a global network of events which are known and experienced simultaneously all over the world.

As the psychologist Richard Farson has pointed out, the new environment is giving us a more human way of life. Contrary to the anti-utopian writers, such as Huxley, Orwell, and Bradbury, the technological future will not totally devaluate man. In fact, the new technology has made possible a new era of radical humanism in which the personal qualities of human life will be enhanced and developed. We are coming increasingly to realize what machines are for and what men are for and to separate the two. The future man will be valued for his usefulness, and not simply because he can substitute for a machine.

31

The Generation Issue

The rapidity with which the social environment has changed has made differences between the generations inevitable. Adults and young adults have grown up in vastly different worlds. Add to this the fact that half of the present population in the United States is under twenty-five years of age. The young adult population is increasing more rapidly than any other age group in our society. The differences between the generations have been increased also by the rise of a dominant young adult culture. It is a unique historical fact that young people have never been separated into their own social settings in such large numbers. This separatism begins in large urban high schools and continues in multiversities, young adult occupational groups, and in exclusive living communities.

The extent of the "gap" between the generations is difficult to assess. Max Lerner, the social critic, believes that one of the big splits in our society is the gap between the generations and that this split will get bigger before it gets smaller. He believes that the time has come when adults can no longer ignore the younger generation. Traditionally adults are to rule, and youth and young adults are to obey their dictates. Such paternalism is coming to an end, and new social structures will be needed to allow adults and young people to be mutually representative in the determination of public policy.

Mike Nichols has allegorized the popular notion of a generation gap in his beautiful film *The Graduate*. Adults, on one hand, are portrayed as phonies who are caught up in the symbols of success, the accumulation of material goods, and in the perpetuation of their own lost youth. Young adults, on the other hand, are seen as authentic individuals who are very self-conscious, immensely serious, and deeply sensitive to human relations. Particularly noticeable are attempts by middle-class adults to extend their own lives through the successes and accomplishments of their children. The rights of young adults are limited by the ego needs of their parents and the adult world's fear of anyone who shows any evidence of being a nonconformist. All this results in a highly entertaining film in which the generational issues are greatly exaggerated and oversimplified. But at the same time Nichols provides a brilliant portrayal of how compulsive adults are in regard to sex, sociality, and modern gadgetry. The film fails, though, in its generalization that all adults are "bad guys" and all young adults are "good guys." It is this kind of myth the popularizers of the generation gap have tended to foster.

Some research tends to play down the differences between generations. One study found that differences were greater between young adults of differing social settings than between young adults and their parents.[19] In other words, social strata, social character, and family background are as significant as age in understanding social differences.

The basic social struggle today is actually not so much an age struggle as a characterological struggle or the attempt to find a social identity compatible with the new social environment. Although some young adult types are the *avant-garde* leaders in such a search, not all young adults

[19] A study by the Center for Research and Development in Higher Education at Berkeley and reported in the *University Bulletin* of the University of California, August 28, 1967, p. 1.

nor even the majority of young adults are involved. Similarly, most adults are more easily identified with the declining social character. But at the same time there are parents and adults who because of background, social setting, and personal openness have joined with the younger generation in finding more relevant ways to live as human beings in our changing world. To conclude that *only* young adults have been touched by the new environment would be an error. The dynamic nature of the last twenty years has actually increased the dynamic nature of all of life, including the adult generation.

The shift in social character does not take place suddenly, nor is it limited to any one age group or social type. It is a process that takes place over a period of time and at various levels in the society. As David Riesman has observed, within any given situation "one may find groups representing all phases of the population curve," and there are a "variety of characterological adaptations to each particular phase." [20] The generational issue therefore may best be understood as the rise of a new man and the decline of the old one. Although the struggle may come to focus primarily between age groups, it cannot be limited to age alone. Throughout the population there are a variety of character types, representing both the new and the old eras. Referring to characterological struggles in general, Riesman writes:

> These character types, like geological or archaeological strata, pile one on top of the other, with outcrop-

[20] *The Lonely Crowd* (Garden City, N.Y.: Doubleday & Co., 1950), p. 49.

pings of submerged types here and there. A cross section of society at any given time reveals the earlier as well as the later character types, the earlier changed through the pressure of being submerged by the later.[21]

We can conclude therefore that the generational gap is a reality, but a reality enhanced, not entirely by age differences, but by the larger issue of what it means to be man in the new age. With this fact established we can now turn to some of the more important issues between the generations.

1. In times of rapid change normal differences between the generations are aggravated and greatly magnified. This is due largely to a breakdown in communication structures between the generations and the inability of society to maintain little if any continuity between the age groups. If the opportunity for one generation to observe another is decreased, then each generation turns in upon itself for social definition. This kind of social phenomenon is presently taking place with the young adult generation. The present structures of society are designed not to enhance communication between the generations, but to separate one generation from another. In such separation not only do subcultures arise, but their importance is exaggerated out of proportion to the larger society. In separate subcultures age groups develop their own values, ways of living, and modes of human expression. The young adult subculture today tends to be an exclusive culture with social barriers; it limits the opportunity for interaction with adults and decreases the possibility of constructive influences being brought to bear by the larger culture.

[21] *Ibid.*

2. Young adults tend to have a limited view of history and are oriented primarily to present "happenings" rather than to events of either the past or the future. McLuhan argues that today's television youth is "attuned to up-to-the-minute" news rather than to things in the past. In fact, young adults are often bewildered when they have to respond to traditional environments where life is ordered, carefully scheduled, and dependable. In the new environment the young adult has learned to live in what President John F. Kennedy described as a state of continued crisis. The result is the young adult generation is much better equipped psychologically to embrace the new and the different with a minimum of threat. In contrast to this, adults tend to look at the present from the point of view of tradition. They cannot understand young adults who have no desire to remain in familiar surroundings, whose entire makeup is to be on the move, and who seemingly have no desire to return to where they once were. Young adults know that the pace of change makes it impossible for them to "go home again." Such a situation has led McLuhan to write what seems to be an apt description of many in the adult generation:

> The past went that-a-way. When faced with a totally new situation, we tend always to attach ourselves to the objects, to the flavor of the most recent past. We look at the present through a rearview mirror. We march backwards into the future. Suburbia lives imaginatively in Bonanza-land.[22]

[22] *The Medium Is the Massage*, pp. 74-75.

3. Another issue is the moral or value gap between the generations. In terms of specific values and moral practices the differences between the generations may not really be as great as we think. A recent study found, for example, that two thirds of the students in the sample felt their sexual attitudes and beliefs were similar to those of their parents.[23] Another study found a high correlation between the attitudes of young adults and their parents on civil rights, the war in Vietnam, and social welfare.[24]

It is entirely possible that the new morality of young adults has been overstated. For half a century morality has become increasingly liberal, moving from rigid standards to flexible guidelines. It is an error to assume that the present young adult generation has been the first to depart from moral tradition. Pragmatism and the humanistic morality of John Dewey set the direction for freeing morality from its religious domination. It is true that this generation of young adults is the first to come of age under the dominant influence of a more humanistic value system.

There are some who feel that this generation of young adults is basically a moral generation. Young adults are more aware of the issues than previous generations and are deeply involved in formulating ways to be morally responsible in the areas of life they feel are important and urgent. The result is that they have emphasized human relationships, the right of individuals to differ, and the importance of personal conscience. A strange contradiction ensues. Young adults have a strong respect for privacy in the per-

[23] Ira L. Reiss, "How and Why America's Sex Standards Are Changing," *Trans-Action*, March, 1968, p. 28.
[24] Center for Research and Development in Higher Education, *op. cit.*

sonal dimensions of the moral life. They are tolerant of the behavior of others and will not pry into the private lives of their peers. On the other hand, they have a strong sense of social justice and are intolerant of an adult society that refuses to be morally responsible in regard to race, war, poverty, and the other social issues of our day.

Another shift that has occurred is in the moral style of young adults. They may not differ much from adults in their beliefs, but they do differ in what they do with their beliefs. The new generation is primarily an activist generation attempting to live out their values in the crucial spots of society. They have become aware of the inconsistencies of adult morality and have responded with a new kind of "moralism" through the way they apply their beliefs. Honesty requires their telling a teacher that his course is "stupid," and love demands personal expression in a kind of naïve romanticism.

Sociologists have sometimes described the dominant middle-class value system as one that is based primarily upon commitments to sociality, materialism, and status. The 1950's were marked largely by social climbing and the accumulation of material goods. Adjustment, getting along with others, and getting ahead were highly prized by adults. In contrast, young adults tend to value individual differences, moral integrity, interpersonal relations, and personal experience. They have adopted a strange combination of existentialism and social activism. The result of this union is a moral style that is in part pervasive, free and yet demanding, rebellious and at the same time constructive. It is a style that is intended to make for a more human life in which love, equality, and freedom might be enjoyed by all.

And as one can readily tell, it has a tinge of utopianism at the cost of reality.

There is growing evidence that the classical differences between the generations are diminishing. Adults are no longer the persons who nurture youth, who know what is best, and whose position demands respect. To a large extent both generations are caught in the same web of change and are mutually dependent upon each other. Respect today is not based upon age, but on the quality of one's life and one's demonstrated competence. There is hope that in the changing roles in our society the gap might be bridged as the generations come to see that both are struggling with the same issue—human survival.

It is true that the young adult generation may point the way to a new way of life. It seems apparent that a new man is emerging and, as Cox has pointed out, this new man will be "a living embodiment of everything the religious, bourgeois individualistic man of the classical Protestant period is not." [25]

[25] *On Not Leaving It to the Snake*, p. 92.

2
Young Adult Culture

One of the most significant developments of the 1960's is the emergence of a prevalent young adult culture. This is something new for American society as youth and young adults in previous generations rarely rejected the larger culture and usually sought their identity in small localized subgroups. There has never been a young adult culture of the magnitude of the present one, and never have young adults belonged with such consciousness to the "whole" of young adulthood.

Today most young adults share a way of life which distinguishes them from other people. Prevalent in this way of life are all the aspects of a culture, such as young adult forms of art, music, symbols, language, life-styles, and attitudes. Culture is also concerned with what it means to be man and, although young adults draw upon the adult culture to a large extent, they are also formulating answers of their own as to what it means to live in an urban-technological world.

The existence of a large peer group culture has resulted in a heightened sense of shared identity and in a reference group to legitimitize the young adult time in life. It serves also to authenticate the capriciousness of young adulthood and to give credence to young adult causes and concerns.

In many ways the young adult culture has all the marks of a minority group that has to exist in opposition to a majority group. Young adults exaggerate in their behavior the rights and privileges identified with adulthood. In extreme ways they act out in dress, sexual gestures, and lifestyles the role of adults which they have yet to achieve. One cannot help detecting a sense of arrogance and self-righteousness as young adults create a defensive mechanism in order to "get even" with or to evade and mislead the adult majority.[1]

A Peer Group Culture

By culture we mean those ideals, symbols, and ways of doing things which are shared by a group of people. The persons who do the sharing make up a society. It is quite obvious from these definitions that young adults belong both to a peer group society and to the larger American society and that they participate to varying degrees in both a peer group culture and the total or universal culture. Bearing this in mind will help us to avoid the popular assumption that young adult culture reflects how far young

[1] Cf. John R. Seeley, *The Americanization of the Unconscious* (New York: International Science Press, 1967), pp. 396-401.

adults have gone in rejecting the larger culture and in developing a separate culture of their own. Actually, it would be more accurate to describe the present young adult culture as a subculture of the culture shared by most persons living in American society.

A critical and scientific approach to the young adult culture will allow several generalizations.

First, we can acknowledge that young adults have rejected certain aspects of the larger culture and have formulated cultural patterns not shared by adults. They reject, for example, the traditional distinctions between masculinity and femininity and have greatly reduced the conventional distance between the sexes by both their actions and outward appearances. The electric sound of young adult music is distinctive to their culture although it is beginning to influence older types of music, particularly the Broadway musical with its static traditionalism.

Second, there is greater continuity between the young adult and the adult cultures than has been popularly perceived. New cultures are formed out of historical events and the process of borrowing from other cultures. To a large extent, young adults share beliefs and values with adults, particularly their parents. In fact, one of the most interesting new developments has been the eagerness with which young adults have reached back into history and remythologized some of the early cultural heroes of American society.

Furthermore, many of the causes supported by young adults are actually the same causes championed by adults which now have been taken up by the younger generation. Chief among these, of course, is the struggle for an integrated society—a theme that dominated the larger culture

42

for at least a decade before students took it up in the late 1950's.

In actuality the young adult culture could not exist apart from the support of adult institutions. The prosperity of our times is a major factor in the development of young adult cultures. Even among the less affluent there are ways of getting the symbols and practicing the rituals of young adulthood—including stealing (borrowing) from the more affluent or using the resources of welfare and social service agencies. Also the adult society provides and even controls the institutions that psychologically support and maintain young adult cultures. Chief among these are educational, military, leisure, and employment structures designed primarily for young adults.

Third, the young adult culture reflects most of the newer themes of the larger culture and its response to the demands of social change. The tolerance which young adults allow for sexual expression has been evolving in the adult society for some time as attested by the Kinsey studies.

Probably more vivid is the extent that the disintegration of the old culture is carried over into the young adult society. The shared forms of protest on the part of young adults are directly related to social ills which adults have long recognized but have not been able to resolve. Probably the major source of conflict between the two cultures is not so much differing values but the priority given to certain values and the methods utilized to achieve them. The basic difference between the generations is that young adults see the older order breaking up and are impatient to get on with the new order. Because the young adult culture is newer, with fewer rigid patterns, it is much more willing to incorporate new themes into its way of life.

Fourth, the evidence seems conclusive that the young adult culture is really an extension of the larger culture and reflects the direction that society is going. Many of the changes and new developments which *seem* to distinguish the young adult culture are actually drawn from the "value pool" of the larger culture. This is not intended to deny that young adults have contributed innovations and new ideas to the larger society. Probably no previous generation has been as productive and creative as the present one. But the young adult culture cannot be interpreted as being primarily a displacement of the adult culture. It is more accurate to describe it as a continuation of themes and patterns that have been developing for some time in the larger culture.

Empirical studies of those persons that might be described as the more exaggerated young adult types, such as dissenters and hippies, conclude that these persons have not abandoned the democratic, humanistic, and permissive attitudes and values of the larger culture. What has happened is that the more traditional norms of the culture have been so fully incorporated into the life-styles of these young adults that they have readily found themselves in conflict with the less democratic and more bureaucratic structures of adult society.[2] The present cultural conflict between the generations is largely related to the young adults' rejection of that part of the middle-class system which allowed all

[2] Edward E. Sampson, "Student Activism and the Decade of Protest," *Journal of Social Issues,* July, 1967, p. 8.

beliefs and values to be tempered by moderation, especially if they might threaten the unity of society or result in conflict. The idealism of the present generation has led young adults to incorporate values into radical patterns of action, some of which are proving destructive to the very institutions designed to serve young adults.

Fortunately, there is now a body of research on the beliefs, values, and patterns of action of young adults. The findings are in general agreement that young adults have not departed basically from the values and norms of the larger society but are expressing them in new and more radical ways. Both Richard Flacks of the University of Chicago and Kenneth Keniston of Yale University found high correlation between the beliefs of young adult protesters and their parents as well as between those held by non-protesters and their parents. There is little evidence, for example, that young adults participating in the various movements of dissent have been converted from, or have rebelled against, values and beliefs held by their parents.[3]

In the Keniston findings there are no signs of a major disjunction between the young adult and the adult cultures. A majority of young adults are not critical of the larger society. Even the activists were in general agreement with parental beliefs and values, although it was felt by some that their parents were sometimes "less-than-sincere" and had often failed to "practice what they preached." At the present time at least young adults tend to live out of the

[3] Richard Flacks, "The Liberated Generation: An Exploration of the Roots of Student Protest," *Journal of Social Issues*, July, 1967, pp. 52-75; Kenneth Keniston, "The Sources of Student Dissent," *ibid.*, pp. 108-135.

"expressed but unimplemented" values of parents.[4] Flacks came to similar conclusions in his study of students primarily from the northern cities. He found that "the great majority of these students are attempting to fulfill and renew the political traditions of their families." [5] Following is a summary statement of his research:

> Whereas nonactivists and their parents tend to express conventional orientations toward achievement, material success, sexual morality and religion, the activists and their parents tend to place greater stress on involvement in intellectual and esthetic pursuits, humanitarian concerns, opportunity for self-expression, and tend to de-emphasize or positively disvalue personal achievement, conventional morality and conventional religiosity.[6]

The American culture for some time has been under the influence of middle-class values and goals. There is much evidence that these are now declining in influence and that humanistic values—those concerned with self-expression and individual development—are increasingly prevailing in much of the culture. The new ethical humanism is certainly reflected in much of the young adult culture, and there are themes and concerns that are shared by many young adults.[7]

To argue that the young adult culture is merely continu-

---

[4] Keniston, "The Sources of Student Dissent," pp. 109, 119. For a more detailed study see his book *The Young Radicals* (New York: Harcourt, Brace & World, 1968).

[5] Flacks, "The Liberated Generation," p. 68.

[6] *Ibid.*

[7] Flacks, "Student Activists: Result, Not Revolt," *Psychology Today,* October, 1967, pp. 18-23.

ing the trends and developments of the larger culture is undramatic, especially for those who enjoy playing up the notion of a major gap between the generations. But the evidence seems clear: The young adult culture reflects the social change that is going on in American society and the reexamination that is taking place in regard to the general system of values and beliefs.

The Cult of Young Adulthood

It must be acknowledged that there are those who perceive the young adult culture as something of a messianic cult. That is, they believe the young adults are not only revolting against the old culture, but they hold the secret of a new way of life that will save traditional society from a toddling old age. Because new generations are supposed to advance civilization, society tends to "overendorse" almost every aspect of a young adult culture. When adults become overly enamored with the causes and life-styles of the young adult generation, they help to create young adult cults.

The tendency in some quarters to celebrate the discontinuities between the young and old cultures and to uncritically endorse the cultic activities of young adults has led to the myth that the new generation possesses some kind of special truth. This has been particularly true of those middle adults who, either because of their own thwarted young adulthoods or because of their alienation from their own peer culture, have overidentified with young adults and in so doing have reinforced the immaturities of the young adults, prolonged their growth toward adulthood, and increased their feelings of self-importance.

47

It is often said that young adults do not want to grow up because it would mean becoming "like adults." But this may speak more of the psychological fears of young adults than about cultural differences. Young adults reflect the inability of modern man to come to grips with human finiteness and to accept the inevitability of aging. The result is a cultic kind of social movement that is more concerned with perpetuating young adulthood than in developing a kind of human society where growing-up is both possible and worthwhile. Jencks and Riesman believe that there are certain real problems in the present tendency of adults to over-identify with young adults. They write, "The danger is that they will also reenforce the incompetent amateurism and the self-indulgent or self-pitying protective cults by which young people so often counteract adult expectations." [8]

The Similarity Myth

Just as misleading is the myth that the present young adult generation is, in reality, not much different than previous generations. "After all," the myth goes, "persons have always had to grow up." Seeley replies indirectly to this point of view by saying that this new generation has become so significant that it has earned distinctive "labels" and become the focal point for numerous articles in the mass-circulated magazines. Today the young adult culture is much like a social organization which requires all young adults to participate. What is novel with this new generation is, according to Seeley, "the degree of participation it demands (in-

[8] "The War Between the Generations," p. 5.

deed makes mandatory), its agenda and credenda, its place, and power vis-à-vis the adult world." [9]

There is another factor which dispels the similarity myth. Adult society is an older generation that is also restless and no longer clear or constant in its beliefs and values. We must remember that the parents of today's young adults were the first to experience fully the loss of tradition and the rise of humanism. Not only has this forced a change in the form and content of young adult rebellion, but it has tended to unite the generations around concerns related to the completion of the humanizing process.

In previous generations young adult rebellion took the form of frivolous activities, such as swallowing goldfish, panty-raids, and sitting on flagpoles. The purpose of most youthful rebellion was to get attention or to playfully provoke adults. In fact, rebellion seldom became more serious than the expected *every-generation* crusade on behalf of free love.

Although the present generation can be very fun-loving and playful, their rebellion tends to be deeply serious, and is directed not so much toward parents or authority figures as against the basic structures of society. For the most part they have selected those concerns which are already big issues for the larger society and have succeeded in turning some low-key social debates into explosive issues. In a society that has been in the habit of expecting playful pranks from its young people, it was a surprise when young adults took up the big causes of education, politics, and international affairs.

[9] *The Americanization of the Unconscious*, p. 397.

49

Parents and other adults in places of responsibility are to a large extent as confused and uncertain about the new times as are their young adult children. Dr. George W. Goethals of Harvard University has argued that in our society a shift has taken place in the myths that define parental roles. Traditionally, parents represented the accumulated experience and knowledge that young people needed in order to avoid some of the pain and anguish of growing up. Parental answers were usually dependable and reflected strongly held beliefs that had stood the test of experience. With such parents a young person's rebellion was explicit as he knew where his parents stood and at what points he was departing from stated positions.

Today parents and most adults are adrift and are no longer sure of themselves. Beliefs and values are fluid, and few of the old answers really match up with the questions that are now being asked. Adults to a large extent are caught in the same changes as the young adult. This has made rebellion more difficult as there are fewer definable positions from which young people can depart from their parents.[10] This is why most rebellion today has shifted its target from parents to the more clearly discernible issues of social injustice, depersonalization, and freedom of expression.

Harbingers of Change

Neither the messianic model that celebrates the discontinuity of the young adult culture nor the repetitious model that emphasizes the recycling of the generations seems adequate to describe the young adult situation today. A third

[10] George W. Goethals, "Adolescence: Variations on a Theme," *Problems of Authority and Identity in the University,* pp. 15-27.

model is here proposed which sees young adults as the harbingers of a changing world. They are the forerunners or the forward wave of the transition that the larger culture is presently experiencing. Incorporated in the young adult culture are all of the positive and negative qualities of a world coming of age. The young adult culture is no more or no less than an extension of the larger culture in a state of profound change.

Dr. Clark Kerr reflects the role of young adults as social harbingers in the following observation regarding the direction that students go in a society.

> The students in any country are usually going in the same direction as the country itself, only the students are a little quicker and go a little bit farther. So if you want to understand students, you better try to understand the country. And also, if you want to understand the country, you better look at the students because they are a very sensitive weather vane that will tell you the way things are pointing.[11]

Deep and far-reaching changes often happen quietly in a society and are undetected until they are made visible by the young. Many of the fundamental changes of a culture are first incorporated in individuals and groups of persons and are only gradually integrated into the total culture in any identifiable way.[12] The present young adult culture serves to make visible the changes which are stirring in the adult society.

[11] Mary Harrington Hall, "Interview with Clark Kerr," *Psychology Today*, October, 1967, p. 27.

[12] Margaret Mead, "Cultural Change and Character Structure," *Identity and Anxiety*, ed. Maurice R. Stein, Arthur J. Vidich, and David Manning White (New York: The Free Press, 1960), pp. 88-98.

Origins of Young Adult Culture

If the young adult culture does not originate in a major disjunction of values and beliefs and is not the result of extensive generational conflicts, then how can we account for its development?

Unfortunately, at this point there are few studies of young adult culture *per se*. Most of our information on the origin of peer-group cultures must be derived from studies of youth, although in many instances the youth culture has been broadly conceived, and reflects the age group we call young adults.

The basic argument is that youth and young adult cultures originate in the growing differentiation of social structures resulting in increased peer group association and interaction. Parsons and White see structural changes of society and not value conflict as the basic cause of youth cultures.[13] David Gottlier arrives at similar conclusions, although he found that shared goals are also a factor in the formation of peer group cultures.[14]

The deep and far-reaching changes described earlier are contributing to an increasing number of specialized social structures which permit, encourage, and even force persons of young adult age into relationships with one another and provide the settings for prolonged interaction. Socialization is shifting from the family and other traditional institutions

[13] Talcott Parsons, *Social Structure and Personality* (New York: The Free Press, 1964), p. 221.

[14] "Youth Subculture: Variations on a General Theme," *Problems of Youth: Transition to Adulthood in a Changing World,* ed. Muzafer Sherif and Carolyn W. Sherif (Chicago: Aldine Publishing Co., 1965), pp. 28-45.

to peer group associations. Although values and goals are drawn from the value pool of the larger society, the peer group is a major force in determining how these are incorporated into life-styles.

Riesman seems to reify the peer group and makes it into a microcosm of the emerging adult culture. For him the peer group has possibly become the major instrument of socialization, especially in the establishment of desires and wants. His argument is well known but it is important to summarize it in relation to young adult culture. He sees society in a historical process of developing from tradition-direction to inner-direction and, eventually, to other-direction. Unlike popular uses of Riesman's typology, he did not understand "other-direction" as resulting in either uniformity of character or social conformity. What he is describing is a change in social character (the shared character of a society or social group) and in the way socialization would take place. American society has moved from traditional man, who is oriented to external controls, to individual man, whose goals and values are "built in" by parents or other adult authorities, to social man, who finds his guidance from his peers. Goals, values, attitudes, and life-styles are fixed externally in the first character type and internally in the second. In the other-directed character type the definition of life is ever shifting and pervasive with the peer group remaining constant as the socializing agency.[15]

The fact of a young adult culture has been enhanced and reinforced by two major developments. The first is the commercialization of young adult life-styles. The *mod,*

[15] *The Lonely Crowd.*

the *hip*, and the *psychedelic* look have been copied, manu-
factured, and distributed as sources of identity not only
for young adults but for the adults as well. Mass media
have not only helped to create the young adult culture, but
have also contributed to what might be described as the
"think-young generation." Much of the young adult culture is spreading in influence among the older generation.
For example, the Ford Mustang was originally developed
to appeal to the growing young adult market. But within a
few years the average owner was a person in his mid-40's.
It is a cultural fact that adults today are much more inclined to look to young adults for styles and fads rather
than developing their own.

A second development has been the contribution of mass
media in *re-presenting* young adult life and in expanding
the culture across regional and class boundaries. Young
adults are not only more visible, but are also more united
around common images, symbols, and other forms of cultural identity. Television, radio, and young-adult-type
magazines are major instruments of acculturation, influenc-
ing life-styles and living patterns and serving as channels
for linking young adults together into a cultural system.
Not only is there much more awareness of themselves as
persons among young adults today but there is social self-
consciousness on the part of the total generation. As never
before in history, young adults have a sense of pride about
being young and a loyalty to what is "their" generation.

Seeley has described the situation this way: "No longer
is it a matter of a gang or group, or even a linkage of groups
in a circumscribed territory, but something much more like

a *people* to which one belongs, and of which the persons actually present are only local exemplars." [16]

Young Adult Subcultures

Because of the necessity to generalize regarding an age group, the impression is left in most discussions that young adults are one undifferentiated cultural group. There are probably some bases for believing that young adults are more alike than different. Douvan and Adelson's study of adolescent groups found that there was a lack of "impressive differences" between young people in American society.[17] As does the larger society, the young adult culture reflects the growing universality of life. In many respects the present young adult generation is more homogeneous than the generations of the 40's and 50's. Typological studies locate the bulk of the young adult population in the center with the exaggerated subgroupings falling to the left and right. The young adults that can be typed "conventional" generally share the same value systems and reflect more of the direction that middle-class society seems to be heading. But at the same time, as a group they pick up the trends and directions of the exaggerated subgroups much earlier than the larger culture and incorporate them more readily into their way of life. The political activists have been a minority group in the young adult culture, reflecting possibly no more than 5 to 10 percent of the total. It is often easy for the adult society to dismiss such minorities

---

[16] *The Americanization of the Unconscious,* p. 397 (italics added).
[17] Elizabeth Douvan and Joseph Adelson, *The Adolescent Experience* (New York: John Wiley & Sons, 1966), p. 345.

as radical, but what they fail to see is that there is more connection between the exaggerated subgroups and the large conventional group than appears at first on the surface. [The subgroupings on the edge of the larger young adult culture establish the issues and set the style that young adults will often incorporate into their culture in more modified forms.]

For example, the political activists are often viewed by the larger society as "kooks" or "misfits." But in actuality they come from the leadership pool of the age group, are high academic achievers, are deeply committed to humanistic values, and represent middle- to upper-middle-class families. There is little doubt that the political involvement of a minority is having its impact upon the larger young adult population. During the 1968 presidential campaign a decisive shift in the usual political apathy of young adults was noted. A Gallup poll revealed that young adults are presently as interested in politics as middle-age adults and much more interested than the older voters. Four persons in ten or 41 percent of the sample expressed willingness to work actively in a political party. Only 4 percent of the total reported no interest whatsoever in politics.[18]

It is entirely possible to conclude that the more extreme young adult types do represent some concerns and interest of the larger cross section of young adults. It is probably also true that the more conventional young adults will find more moderate ways to demonstrate concern for the issues

[18] George Gallup, "Political Action and U. S. Youth," *Los Angeles Times*, April 7, 1968.

that the more active members of his peer group have articulated in extreme forms.

To argue that the age group reflects universal themes and ideals is not to say that it is becoming more uniform. Although a majority share a common cultural identity, there is also a wide variance in the way young adults express themselves. It would be equally true that the generation reflects the growing pluralism of contemporary society.

The classical studies of youth and young adult subcultures focused primarily upon the variations between social classes and ethnic groups. That such variations continue to exist, particularly in the private or personal dimensions of life, is attested by several recent studies of young adult behavior. But these distinctions are no longer as sharp and as important as they were during the first quarter of this century when minorities and foreign immigrants poured into the cities. Region, religion, and race are no longer major determinants of identity for young adults, and these young people are generally able to cross most of the social boundaries with little difficulty. The major exception is the Negro, who may be caught in the black ghetto more than ever before. And yet there is much leveling taking place between the races, and those who do escape the ghetto readily participate in the shared identity of the generation.

Cultural pluralism today is due not so much to sociological boundaries as to the increased options which mass communications and technology provide. There is a greater variety of models for human life available to the young adult, and there are fewer structured demands placed upon personal expression. The young adult is much freer to innovate and to experiment, a fact which naturally contributes to pluralism in cultural forms.

The variations in young adult subcultures seem to center primarily in the life styles and behavioral patterns shared by subgroupings of young adults. Differences between the various subgroups are probably related to several factors.

1. Young adult subcultures probably have their roots as much in the search for identity as in the causes that the young adults supposedly represent. There is inherent in the young adult developmental stage a need to find a definition for one's life. Such a definition requires a cause to which a person can give himself, and which will give identity to one's life. An example of this point is the Black Power movement which serves both as a cause and as a means for establishing an identity of worth for a social group that has experienced great diffusion and depersonalization because of color. The bohemian, the playboy, the sophisticate, the bachelor girl, the dissenter, and the military are some of the movements by which young adults try to find a personal identity for life.

For most young adults identity arises after much experimentation, and it is not unusual for an individual to belong to several subcultures at the same time or to progressively move from one group to another.

2. The extent to which persons accept or reject prevailing social institutions is another factor in the formation of subcultures. Richard Peterson has formulated a typology to show that there are six categories of young adults, ranging from those who give uncritical acceptance to prevailing

social institutions to those who make almost full rejection of them.[19]

The *vocationists* in Peterson typology are the young adults who come primarily from the working classes and who are eager to establish themselves in the American system and, if at all possible, to climb socially and economically. Because their personal goals are related to the traditional American dream, they generally accept uncritically society as it is and deny that far-reaching changes are taking place. Falling about the same place in the typology are the *professionals* who also accept society pretty much as it is. They are young adults who are well endowed intellectually, who are highly motivated to success in the professions, and who come from families of high achievement. Although basically conservative politically they are inclined to "play it cool," to not get involved, and to support the *status quo*.

Standing one step beyond full acceptance of the prevailing social system, but not remaining entirely neutral, are the *collegiates*. These are the stereotype of the fun-loving college student or the typical playboy. They are the pleasure-seekers who become critical of the social system only when it interferes with their hedonistic desires. Coming primarily from middle- to upper-middle-class backgrounds, the collegiates collect the symbols of success

[19] "The Student Left in American Higher Education," *Daedalus*, Winter, 1968, pp. 299-308. Peterson's typology is an adaptation of Burton R. Clark and Martin Trow, "The Organizational Context," *College Peer Groups*, ed. Theodore M. Newcomb and Everett K. Wilson, (Chicago: Aldine Publishing Co., 1966). Gottlier also relies on Clark and Trow in "Youth Subculture: Variations on a General Theme," pp. 34 ff.

rather than putting efforts into what the symbols represent. In this regard the diploma and not educational achievement is the goal. The collegiates are oriented generally toward getting along with and manipulating others. Politically they are conservatives although they generally do not believe that most issues are worth their getting involved.

In the center of the typology and remaining largely neutral toward the prevailing social system are what Peterson calls the *ritualists*. These are the young adults who go through the routine of schooling, work, and other social demands and remain generally unexcited and basically noncommittal to everything. The ritualists generally come from the lower socioeconomic strata, believe that they have little influence, and are apolitical and unconcerned about the society and its problems.

Moving toward the left but situated just beyond center are the *academics*. Oriented to scholarly achievements, these are the "eggheads," who are more interested in research and scholarship than in activism. Avoiding extensive involvements and practical issues, this group of young adults is generally sympathetic toward the reform movements. Moving toward the left even more and remaining generally very critical of the prevailing social system are the *intellectuals*. These are the young adults who come from liberal backgrounds and who have had broad experiences in the process of growing up. Instead of being narrow scholars, they are men with an educational attainment which is quite broad with an emphasis upon ideas and the integration of disciplines rather than upon specialization and research. They are not as motivated toward scholarship as the academics and are almost compulsive in their need to be in step with the times and to maintain the "right" outlook.

At the edge of the rejection spectrum are the *left-activists* and the *hippies*. The left-activists are deeply committed to causes that are critical of the prevailing social system and are generally deeply involved in social and political action. They prefer to work in *ad hoc* organizations as they do not trust the established structures and have little confidence that any reform is possible through traditional institutions. Left-activists come from prosperous families and have parents who are liberal and humanitarian in outlook. This group shares similar ideas with the intellectuals, but is much more outraged by the hypocrisy and injustices of society and is more quickly moved to flagrant rejection of law and order. Most left-activists believe that society is so evil that only extreme methods of change can be effective in bringing about any correction.

The *hippies* are the young adults who are most thoroughgoing in their rejection of the social values and institutions of society. Although they would like to see reform, they do not believe that anything can really be done to make the situation better. They believe that the only way to improve society is to create communes where love can be shared in deeply personal ways. Because they come from families who can support them financially, these young adults reject the prevailing society almost totally and withdraw into primitive forms of human existence.

3. A third way to categorize subcultures is according to social alienation. Keniston's study of student dissenters has resulted in a typology that would be applicable to the

young adult population. On a continuum he establishes two ideal types: the *political activist* and the *culturally alienated*. The first represents those young adults who turn outward to society, and the second refers to those young adults who turn inward to themselves. In Keniston typology the *political activists* are oriented primarily outward to the injustices of society and the need to cause change to occur. The *culturally alienated* are those who withdraw from society into their own personal world in order to enhance their experiences and to expand their emotional lives.

The activists are concerned primarily with *ad hoc* issues and structures and choose those methods of reform that will shock the adult society and bring issues into the open. The alienated group adopts styles of nonconformity, especially in dress and behavior patterns. They tend to drop out of conventional society in order to cultivate the sensuous and aesthetic qualities of life.

Keniston compares the two groups in the following way.

> Alienated students tend to be drawn from the same general social strata and colleges as protesters. But psychologically and ideologically, their backgrounds are often very different. Alienated students are more likely to be disturbed psychologically; and although they are often highly talented and artistically gifted, they are less committed to academic values and intellectual achievement than are protesters.[20]

[20] "The Sources of Student Dissent," p. 113. See also his longer study, *The Uncommitted* (New York: Harcourt, Brace & World, 1965).

4. It is possible to adapt Keniston typology to portray another source of subgroupings. On a continuum ranging from individualistic concerns to public concerns a series of ideal types can be established. Among those subgroups that are turned primarily inward in order to achieve personal satisfaction or to serve individual desires are the *leisure* groups. These are the young adult hedonists, who are concerned primarily with having as much fun and in realizing as much personal pleasure as possible. The playboys, playmates, bachelor clubs of various kinds, hippies, and drug-oriented groups would be some examples. The *church* types are those young adults who are basically afraid of the world or who do not like modern urban society and thus use religion as an escape and as a way of reinforcing personal prejudices and hang-ups. These are represented by the Eastern religious cults, the Ayn Rand types, young adult church groups, Campus Crusade, and various spiritualists and mystic orders.

Moving toward the social would be the various *political* organizations for young adults, including young Republicans and Democrats, campus-church groups, and moderate groups like the League of Women Voters. These groups are more ideologically oriented than action-oriented. They spend a great deal of time studying issues, with action occurring primarily through established structures. The more socially oriented groups are the *actionists*. These are such groups as the Black Student Union, Students for Democratic Action, social reformers, and the church renewalists. These are the young adults who are primarily oriented to issues rather than to ideas or organizations.

A typology is only an analytical tool and does not represent labels for individuals. We have looked here at some "ideal" types in order to demonstrate that the young adult culture is composed of one age group that has found a variety of expressions. It is sometimes easy to "pigeonhole" young adults and overlook the fact that most of them belong to more than one subculture and change their basic orientation several times in the process of growing up. The importance of young adult culture is to see that in our society today we have an age group that is dominant in its influence and involved in most of the major issues which mark our time. Most of all, the young adult culture is evidence that there is a "life in our times" that can be described as young adulthood.

3

Religion and Morality

In the preceding chapters we have argued for what some might call the "conventionality" of young adults. There are two reasons for this. First, the empirical data that is available points strongly toward a greater continuity between the generations than has been popularly perceived. Second, in spite of the growing influence of a peer-group culture, individuals bring to young adulthood beliefs and values learned from parents and other significant adults. It is probably not an over-statement to suggest that young adults do not create beliefs and values as much as they take up the assumptions created by adults.

This is not to deny that society is experiencing a major upheaval and that almost every aspect of human life is changing. Nowhere is this more apparent than in the way traditional beliefs and values are now being questioned. Probably not since the Protestant Reformation have religion and morality been subject to such extensive debate and attempts at reformulation.

But before we become too extreme in our description of life in these times, we need to remind ourselves that a total displacement of traditional belief and morality has not taken place—even within the young adult culture. When older assumptions begin to crumble before new ideas, there are always those fearful minorities who turn to the traditional in greater dedication. They do this either because the new ideology is threatening their sense of identity or because it represents social changes that will result in their loss of status and position. Beliefs and values are so closely related to the identity of a group that a social "backlash" is inevitable whenever those concepts are threatened. For example, the increasing hostility of some whites toward the new black identity is due partly to the Negro's rejection of the assumptions behind a white middle-class identity. The black man no longer believes that white is a superior color and is the standard for beauty, success, and power. The rise of new blackness in our society has not only questioned the worth of whiteness, but has also called into question the value systems which supported white as a superior symbol for human life. The very roots of white middle-class identity have thus been challenged.

The Ideological Revolution

A revision in religious and moral beliefs seldom takes place within a brief span of history. This is why most individuals within a particular culture will combine in varying degrees the assumptions of both the new and old orders.

To affirm that the old does not easily fade away does not depreciate the fact that religious and moral revolutions are taking place. It is to point out that a revolution is both the process of building up new beliefs and values and downgrading the older ones.[1] At the moment in our culture, more tearing down than building up may be taking place.

In spite of the apparent conventionality of much of it, the young adult culture provides some clear indications that new assumptions are emerging. Young adults also provide the function of downgrading older beliefs and values by calling society's attention to the fact that they are no longer relevant. Dissent and other forms of disaffection are signs that the middle-class system may be losing its influence. Almost undetected, new themes and ideals have emerged to influence and shape urban man's way of life. Traditional religion apparently is losing its influence, and formal morality is giving way to more flexible and pragmatic styles of moral behavior.

The decline of the middle-class system marks also the wane of its source, the Protestant ethic with its emphasis upon achievement, self-control, and conformity. As we shall see, the attitudes which are now emerging are concerned with personal expressiveness, self-development, and the social welfare of others. The shift is from established prescriptions for human conduct to individual and social development in which creativity, uniqueness, and situational answers are valued.

These shifts in the assumptions and goals for human life have undoubtedly been going on for some time. As most

[1] Seeley, *The Americanization of the Unconscious,* p. 15.

studies suggest, the shift in attitude has far exceeded any major shifts in social practices. Society has grown increasingly tolerant of the new although most members continue to live—at least publicly—in conventional ways. This is probably because private behavior changes faster than public behavior.

The philosopher William Barrett believes the decline in religion has been taking place for some time, possibly for at least three hundred years. He indicates that the rise of rationalism and the scientific method have increasingly contributed to the secularization of society.[2] The present young adult generation is unique in that it is only the first generation to feel the full impact of the scientific and technological revolution, but it is also the first to be nurtured completely under the influence of the social sciences, mainly psychology and sociology. The result is that young adult beliefs and values are deeply personalistic and humanitarian. Young adults are intensely aware of their own needs as well as the needs of others.

Probably just as significant is that they are the first generation to grow up with "modern" parents. Today's young adults have been described as "postmodern" as they reflect the breaks with tradition which their parents made. This probably accounts for the close kinship which most parents and young adults enjoy and for the great tolerance and understanding which society brings to the present young adult unrest. It is also further evidence that the generation gap is actually more a characterological struggle than a conflict between parents and young people. Parents

[2] *Irrational Man* (Garden City, N. Y.: Doubleday & Co., 1958), pp. 20-36,

of this new generation were among the first to break the shackles of supernatural religion and Victorian morality and to embrace the tenets of the new psychology, the New Deal, and the new religion of the Social Gospel. Liberal parents have given rise to a much more emancipated young adult generation, dedicated to translating parental principles into social practices.

Stanley Kramer's film *Guess Who's Coming to Dinner* illustrates our point. The film portrays a crusading newspaper publisher and his equally liberal wife, who return home from Hawaii to discover with much shock that their daughter plans to marry a Negro. The daughter, in turn, finds it unbelievable that her parents would oppose the marriage because they have always championed liberal causes, such as integration, human equality, and personal freedom. Although the film has been widely billed as a story on the generation gap, the real issue in the story is what happens when young adults decide to translate parental values into the ordinary ventures of life. In this case, the result was the possibility of an interracial marriage.

It is convenient to point to the more visible and articulate young adults as examples of how much the new generation has broken with tradition. But it may be that the themes and ideals of a few have impregnated a larger cross section of young adults than we have acknowledged. Quite possibly the new humanitarian tradition has extended much further into the conventionality of young adult life than has outwardly been revealed. Many middle-class families are not willing to risk the security of status and position to take up political causes, but they are nevertheless open to those beliefs and values that will give new shape to the private dimensions of life. A study of young Catholics, for example, revealed extensive disenchantment with the organized church. Also, it is well substantiated that middle-class Catholics disagree in attitude and practice with the church's stand on birth control.[3]

Probably even more far reaching in implication is the present status of religious institutions in middle-class society. On one hand, the church in suburbia has all the appearance of a strong and influential institution. But upon closer examination, we find that the church is established in middle-class communities because it is "a good influence in the community," because it "helps to maintain property values," and for "the sake of the children." As Barrett points out, religion is supported primarily because it is good for the "national interest" which is a clear indication "that in the modern world the nation-state, a thoroughly secular institution, outranks any church."[4] Evidently religion is not as influential even among conventional young adults as is often believed.

The declining influence of religion is substantiated by three trends. The first is the downward spiral of church membership, especially among the major denominations. For several years church membership has not kept up with population growth, and for the last two years many denominations have registered significant losses. Along with the losses in membership has come an even greater drop in the number of persons who attend worship services or

[3] "The Faith of the Youth: An Emerging Problem," editorial in *America*, July 16, 1966, p. 54.
[4] *Irrational Man*, p. 21.

participate in church schools, youth and young adult groups, and other programs of the churches.

Second, a Gallup Poll reports organized religion has steadly lost influence in American society. Ten years ago a poll found that 69 percent of the sample felt that religion was gaining in influence, while only 14 percent felt it was declining in influence. Today, a similar poll found that only 23 percent believed religion was increasing in influence, while 57 percent felt it was declining in influence.

The third trend is the growing dissatisfaction in the church of ministers, particularly those under forty years of age. A survey of three thousand Protestant clergymen, published by *McCall's* magazine, found that not only were clergymen angry with the church, but almost half of those under forty reported that they had considered leaving the ministry.[5] If this is the attitude of young adults who are in the ministry of the church, it might be safe to generalize that other young adults are disaffected in even greater numbers.

The Religious Situation

Harvey Cox has said that the "collapse of traditional religion" is one of the two major characteristics of our age. The other being urbanization and the way men live together.[6] Barrett has written that the decline of religion is much more than an intellectual crisis; it represents a major psychological crisis for man. Religion for traditional man was the matrix in which he lived and expressed himself.

[5] Reported in "Antidote to Despair," *Together*, April, 1968, p. 17.
[6] *The Secular City*, p. 1.

Today's man has given up religion and its transcendentalism in order to confront directly the natural order as it is. The result is that "religion is no longer the uncontested center and ruler of man's life and the church is no longer the final and unquestioned home and asylum of his being." [7] This has resulted in a new religious situation in our society.

1. The religious situation in which young adults find themselves is first of all a secular situation. This means that religion has not only declined in the affairs of men, but it does not provide the primary norms and sanctions for ordering life. That the forms of religion remain in our society is certainly true; however, these forms to a large extent are "museum pieces" in nature, being preserved as a memory of the past rather than a witness to the present.

As Martin Marty has suggested, secularization is being established at a rapid pace in the West as we experience a movement toward "a new style of godless man, a self-engrossed and self-interpreting world, a cosmos in which the 'god of explanation' is absent and in which notes of transcendence and mystery are disappearing." [8] In short, young adults are coming of age in a time in which society seems to be turning from other worlds to the natural world and to this present age for the context and orientation of human life.

2. In the second place, the religious situation today, for many at least, is not heresy (false belief) or even disbelief (caring, but not being able to accept). Rather it is

[7] *Irrational Man*, p. 21.
[8] "The Religious Situation: An Introduction," *The Religious Situation: 1968*, ed. Donald R. Cutler (Boston: Beacon Press, 1968), p. xxi.

72

primarily *unbelief*, that is, not caring enough to ask the questions of belief. Such a situation seems almost a contradiction in a society in which over 90 percent acknowledge some kind of recognition of a supreme being. Surveys suggest there is no more than 1 or 2 percent of the population who are confirmed atheists. My own interpretation of the situation is that it has become much easier to blandly accept God along with the other symbols of good citizenry than to have to struggle with the intellectual quest for understanding. In spite of the recent brief flurry over the "God-is-dead" theology (which was really a responsible intellectual quest), there is little evidence that contemporary man even knows what the religious questions are for today.

3. The religious situation is also marked by what Michael Novak calls the "collapse of folk religion." By folk religion Novak means "a modality of religious life whose strength derives from family sentiment, local customs, and national inheritance; negatively, a modality whose strength does not come from the drive to raise questions." [9]

In a real sense, we in America have tried to make everything into a religion. From almost the beginning of the nation religion was disestablished and made a part of the American way of life. Slogans were coined, such as "In God We Trust"; and allegiance to God became synonymous with allegiance to the nation. Religious beliefs were incorporated into the myths regarding our national leaders. Even more essential was the assumption that success was

[9] "The New Relativism in American Theology," *The Religious Situation: 1968*, p. 208.

a sign of faith and failure marked the unfaithfulness of a man's relationship to God.

The "religionization" of American life is nowhere more clearly exemplified than in the way the public schools have used prayers, scripture readings, and religious observances to indoctrinate the young into a generalized American religion. In fact, many young adults' stereotypes of religion were influenced more by the generalized religion of public schools than by the historical theology of particular churches. It is interesting to observe that in whatever way the generalized religion was passed from generation to generation, it was marked primarily by personal piety and devotional exercises and not by intellectual and theological integrity.

4. To a large extent young adults have grown up in a religious situation that has psychologized religious beliefs and practices. Allport has described this type of religious motif as "psychologism." By this he means that the principles and meanings for life along with the goals for human personality are derived decreasingly from historical tenets of faith and are taken more and more from psychology, psychiatry, and mental hygiene.[10]

The last two decades have witnessed the popularization of the psychological interpretation of religious beliefs and practices, and all too often psychological premises were preached and taught without any attempt to correlate them with religious tradition. Programs of religious education and other forms of the church's work reflected greatly the impact of psychology, and emphasis was placed upon

[10] Gordon W. Allport, *The Individual and His Religion* (New York: The Macmillan Co., 1951), p. 2.

74

character development, personal adjustment, and mental and emotional health. The church became increasingly a mental hygiene center under the cover of religious justification.

In spite of the many contributions derived from this trend, several negative results can be identified. First, personalistic psychology tended to reinforce the themes of personal piety characteristic of the evangelical movement. Psychological norms replaced religious norms and served only to continue the uniformity of religious expression. Psychological moralism was substituted for puritan moralism. Even more serious, the psychologizing of religion resulted in heightening the middle-class style of modern Protestantism with its emphasis upon personal adjustment, self-improvement, and social conformity.

5. Like most of modern society, the religious situation today is marked by several contradictions. One of these is that at the very time religion seems to be waning, there are also signs of a religious revival. One commentator has remarked that it is surprising to find so many people interested in the death of religion. Second only to sex, religion has occupied the attention of secular man in the mid-1960's. But it is difficult to tell if this interest is what young adults call "camp," a fad out of the past, or a kind of objective diversion on the part of man to inform himself on the times. Quite possibly Jerald C. Brauer of Chicago Divinity School is correct when he says that all men are basically religious and that when they cannot find satisfaction in one religion, they will turn to another.

Undoubtedly the religious situation today is closely related to the larger cultural crisis in which men are seeking to understand their situation and to find the meaning that will let them rise above it. The loss of religion may be only the decline of outmoded forms of religious institutionalism. There is extensive evidence that modern man is in a quest for understanding that will transcend the temporal situation in which he finds himself. Such a search seems to be taking place today largely within secular structures. This is what Joseph Campbell describes as the "secularization of the sacred." By this he means that the profane experiences of life contain the possibility of religious awe and a confrontation with the sacred.[11] Not only is this style of religious life represented in much of contemporary theology, but it is basic to such fads as the hippie movement. Probably nowhere has the possibility of a religious revival been more apparent than in the preoccupation of the intellectual community with Oriental religion, with its emphasis upon transcendentalism and the expansion of the mind in order that the individual may grasp more of himself as well as the reality which surrounds the self.

Beliefs and Practices

Young adults are generally less interested in formal religion than any other age group. They are at an age when they declare their independence by rejecting the religious beliefs and practices of their parents.[12] It is a time of moratorium in which they not only question the beliefs and moral values which their parents have taught, but they also

[11] "The Secularization of the Sacred," *The Religious Situation: 1968*, p. 601.

[12] Allport, *The Individual and His Religion*, p. 37.

determine to remain free from any binding commitments. Young adulthood can be characterized as that stage in life in which persons must search for an ideology or a system of meanings that will serve to establish their identity as they become adults.

Allport believes that in spite of the rejection of formal religion on the part of young adults, there remains at this time in life a strong disposition toward the religious.[13] As a part of the developmental process, there emerges in the young adult a strong impulse to give himself to a cause and to serve a purpose which is larger than the self. The search for meaning and worthy purposes arises in the normal growth patterns of moving from the egocentricity of adolescence to the allocentricity of adulthood. In fact, classical psychology of religion tells us that the experience of doubt and questioning in young people is the psychological basis for what we used to describe as religious conversion. In our time conversion is marked not so much by a radical religious experience as by a gradual unfolding of meaning and the commitment to a cause.

The tragedy is that so many young adults never allow themselves to question beliefs or to be confronted with the searching demands of life in order that their religious clichés and moralisms can be fully examined. As Allport points out, there is probably no region of the personality that claims "so many residues of childhood as . . . the religious attitudes of adults." [14] For all too many young adults it is not a loss of faith which besets them but a superficial faith which reinforces pietism and provides a

[13] *Ibid.*, pp. 36 ff.
[14] *Ibid.*, p. 52.

shelter from the searching demands of life. It is the fortunate person who in the process of growing up experiences a religious reorientation and finds a new openness to religion and the commitments for life which it provides.

Today most young adults find religion remote and unrelated to their life needs. In fact, most studies indicate that the prevailing mood is not so much rebellion or rejection as it is apathy. Religion has not been for most young adults a vital influence in their growing up nor a significant factor in the lives of their parents. The result is a generation that is less inclined toward religion and much more secularly oriented.[15] This reflects not only the general mood of the adult society, but a continuation of an attitude strongly held by the parents of this generation.

We need to recall once again that these parents were young adults themselves during and following World War II. Research studies conducted during that period indicate that in spite of claims of a religious revival and reported increases in church membership there was only a moderate interest in religion on the part of young adults. In 1950, Murray G. Ross published a study on religious beliefs of persons between the ages of 18 and 29. Using a population sample drawn from YMCA's and from regions generally conservative religiously, Ross found a growing disinterest in religion. Although a majority indicated they held religious beliefs, only one tenth could specify what these beliefs were. Furthermore, less than 20 percent found their religion providing a basis for their daily life, and 50 percent admitted that they never discussed religion. Four out of five

[15] Douglas Heath, "*The Cool Ones,*" an unpublished paper reporting research on college students.

considered themselves nominal church members, and half this number claimed to have attended church weekly. But when the interviewer asked later how many had attended church services within the past week, only 33 percent answered in the affirmative.[16]

Similar conclusions were reached by Allport in his study of the postwar student generation. He found an inclination on the part of students to be religious, but not very formal in the development of a religious life. Over half of the students had repudiated the church of their parents. Although most of the students held theistic beliefs, they were either unorthodox in their interpretation or were unable to make any interpretations. Allport concluded that the students in his study had almost no comprehension of historical religion and were theologically illiterate.[17]

In general we can conclude that the parents of the present young adult generation broke with orthodoxy, embraced religious liberalism, and to a large extent dropped out of churches. Although they formally held church membership, the number actively involved was lower than the other age groups after the war. It might be argued that they returned to the church when they became parents, but the evidence seems to suggest that even then the majority established only a marginal relationship.

Disinterest in the church has increased over the last twenty years. The first evidence we have is that greater numbers of young adults have disengaged themselves from adult-oriented institutions, including the church, in recent years. A study made in the early 1960's found that although

[16] *Religious Beliefs of Youth* (New York: Association Press, 1950).
[17] *The Individual and His Religion*, pp. 36-46.

church membership continued high, only 25 percent were active participants. Less than half this number were participating in the church in any significant degree, with only about 15 percent related in any way as leaders. Generally, young adults desire to be free of commitments and involvement and their disinterest in church seems no different than their disinterest in other community organizations. Eighty percent did not belong to any formal group or organization.[18]

From limited research and reports of participants in young adult subgroups, it is possible to make some cautious generalizations about young adult religious beliefs and practices in the mid-1960's.

1. There is strong evidence that the more alert, intelligent, socially sensitive, and politically aware young adult is less likely to be found in the church.[19] Young people who are leaders in school or other young adult settings are likely not to be active in the church and, if they are, it is on a marginal basis.[20]

2. Churches seem to attract young adults from high-status families with above-average income. In other words, churches are more oriented to families that are traditionally middle class.[21] Also, the more fearful, guilt-possessed, and

[18] Allen S. Ellsworth, *Young Men and Young Women: New Insights on Becoming Adult* (New York: National Council of the Young Men's Christian Association, 1963), especially p. 50.

[19] William A. Watts and David Whittaker, "Free Speech Advocates at Berkeley," *Journal of Applied Behavioral Science*, II, 1968, 41-62.

[20] Robert J. Havighurst, *et al.*, *Growing Up in River City* (New York: John Wiley & Sons, 1962), pp. 94-95.

[21] *Ibid.*

unadjusted people may find their way to the church in greater number than the less inhibited and more liberated and open young adults. The more intellectually oriented persons as well as young adults from low-income and impoverished backgrounds are not found in churches.

3. There is a correlation between the religious beliefs and practices of young adults and their parents.[22] Most young adults do acknowledge themselves to be religious, and ascribe their beliefs to their parents, but they have little understanding of what they believe and almost no ability to articulate religious beliefs.[23]

4. The more politically and socially active young adults are, the less likely they are to be members of churches or to acknowledge historical systems of belief. Studies indicate that student activists tend to see themselves as nonreligious, and in fact they have long been free from religious traditions. A comparison between activists and a cross section of students found that 61 percent of the activists never attended church as compared with 25 percent of the cross section. To state the findings positively, nearly 8 percent of the activists attend church services with some regularity as compared with 22 percent of the cross section. But even more significantly, those in neither group felt that religion had much influence on their lives and saw little relation between religion and some of the more significant ethical issues. Although the activists were generally very liberal in their religious beliefs, the cross section also revealed strong tendencies to be in-

[22] Watts and Whittaker, "Free Speech Advocates at Berkeley."
[23] James W. Trent and Judith L. Craise, "Commitment and Conformity in the American College," *Journal of Social Issues*, July, 1967, p. 37.

fluenced by secular beliefs rather than by historical religious formulations.[24]

5. There is a widespread revival in the study of religion on the part of young adults. This is especially apparent on state college and university campuses where the religion departments are fast becoming popular. This interest by young adults is probably due to the declining influence of the church in their lives, their desire to question and evaluate the beliefs and values of religious tradition, and their being given an opportunity to seriously explore religious alternatives without being confronted with the possibility of making a commitment. The evidence suggests that in spite of the large number of students enrolling in religious courses, there is no great shift toward historical religion or participation in the churches.[25]

New Religions

William Hamilton is reported to have said that no one over thirty will understand the "death-of-God" theology. What he apparently means is that young adults are the ones most aware of the loss of historical belief in contemporary society and most open to the new religious alternatives.

Americans in every generation have been particularly susceptible to religious fads and bizarre spiritual movements. We have had our Aimée Semple McPhersons, all kinds of cults, such as the New Harmony, the Oneida

[24] Watts and Whittaker, "Free Speech Advocates at Berkeley."
[25] Robert A. Spivey, "Modest Messiahs: The Study of Religion in State Universities," Religious Education, January-February, 1968, pp. 5-12.

Community, the I-Am sect, and the various vegetarian movements, socialist experiments, and free-love communities.

Today the religious alternatives include Playboyism (neo-hedonism), Ayn Rand's Objectivism (religion of selfishness), the Diggers (the hippie cult of poverty), Timothy Leary's Neo-Americanism Church (drug cult), Zen Buddhism (spiritual exercises), Maharishi Mahesh Yogi's Spiritual Regeneration Movement (transcendental meditation), and humanistic psychologism (self-discovery and expression).

Religious alternatives always emerge when the established religion has failed to keep in touch with its adherents or when it becomes irrelevant to their deeper needs. This has been the case throughout history. Whenever Christianity failed to satisfy the human longing for meaning and significant experience, man has either formulated his own religion or has adapted the religions of some other tradition. This is what is apparently occurring in our society today. There is an incessant search going on to find the spiritual and to locate the sacred within secular settings.

You might say that we are experiencing a recovery of religion outside the structures of traditional Christianity. In the new religions are certain themes which stand out in spite of the unusual nature of some of the practices surrounding them.

The first is a belief that supernaturalism is dead and that the essence of spirituality lies within the human experience. For many young adults, the "death of God" is an affirmation that God no longer exists beyond or apart from the common ventures of human life. What is emphasized here is the doctrine of incarnation, or the belief in the radical significance of human life in all of its manifestations. It is within the depths of human experience that God is known, and it is the natural experiences of life that have sacramental possibility for spiritual fulfillment. As Huston Smith has pointed out, the basic theme is that "theological supernaturalism is replaced by psychological supernaturalism defined as saving truth available only through altered, turned-on states of consciousness, whether induced by drugs or otherwise." [26]

A second theme is concerned with the recovery of community and the sacredness of relationship. This is nowhere more vividly exemplified than in humanistic psychologism. Not only has the small group become the seat of religious experience, but "Growth Centers" have emerged in many parts of the country to which persons can make regular pilgrimages in order to experience anew a sacramental intimacy of personal encounter.

The concern for community arises out of a middle-class society that has the trappings of togetherness, such as cocktail hours, first-name calling, and personal small talk. In contrast, its emphasis is upon honest and direct encounters at the most elementary levels. As the hippies have dramatized, clothes and other barriers may sometimes need to be discarded in order for people to meet each other with as few disguises as possible. In hippie communes, persons are accepted with no question as to who they are and where they come from. In the sharing of food, work, bed, and love, the experience of community results. As Bon-

[26] "Secularization and the Sacred: The Contemporary Scene," *The Religious Situation: 1968*, pp. 597 f.

hoeffer suggested, community cannot be made—it must come as a gift.

A third theme in the new religions is the quest for the spirit. You might say that in our time a new mysticism has emerged. Rather than attempting to embrace a God who is supernatural and beyond the natural processes of life, the new mystic is attempting to embrace more fully the spirit which is within himself and the life that is all around him. Sometimes the quest of the spirit has turned the mystic to various drugs in an attempt to heighten the experiences of his consciousness. More often it is through one of the various forms of meditation. Zen Buddhism has doubled its adherents in this country within the last three or four years and is becoming firmly established in many of the major cities of the United States. Its appeal seems to be in its premise that realization of the spiritual comes through exercises in meditation that allow a person to experience more fully himself as well as the world around him.

A movement growing in popularity is the Spiritual Regeneration Movement led by the Indian Guru Maharishi. Its emphasis is upon personal meditation which helps one to expand the conscious mind and to embrace more fully the deeper levels of thought. There are meditation groups in most cities and adjacent to most major universities. Presently Maharishi is the highest paid religious lecturer in the world.

The fourth theme is self-expression or personal realization. It is what the hippies call "to do your thing" or what humanistic psychologism refers to as growing in self-understanding and awareness. This means that every individual needs to realize his basic calling, which is to be creative and beautiful in fulfilling his personhood.

The fifth theme is that goodness and evil are relative. What we have here is a rejection of moralism (good conduct for goodness' sake) and legalism (prescribed moral behavior). In almost every one of the new religions an emphasis is placed upon the primacy of love in human affairs rather than upon right or wrong conduct. In the Eastern religions as manifested in America, there is an absence of teachings on morality, sin, and penance.

In looking at these religious alternatives we find it apparent that they are not really new. They have all been tried before and abandoned, although few young adults have enough of a historical perspective to be aware of this fact. Furthermore, it is interesting to observe that many of the themes are actually inherent within the Christian tradition. As one commentator pointed out, the tragedy is not that young adults (and their parents) are rejecting Christianity and Judaism but that they do not know anything about what they have so easily set aside as irrelevant.

On the hopeful side there is evidence that in these religious fads and alternatives are signs of a new religious revival. The search for the spiritual will eventually lead young adults to explore the ingredients of historical Christianity and to do so without the superficial hang-ups of Sunday school teachings and shallow institutionalism. Huston Smith has written that religion is larger than institutional expressions. He writes, "Institutionalized religion isn't all of religion, and the fact that the sacred is withdrawing from certain spheres doesn't mean it isn't moving into others. Robert Bellah could be right in detecting 'in the United States . . . at the moment something of a religious revival.' " [27]

The Moral Situation

It generally believed that each new generation of young adults is less moral than previous generations. Young adults even believe this about themselves, although there is no empirical evidence to support such a belief. In fact, our findings indicate that young adults more likely than not share moral values with their parents. The difference between the two groups is that young adults are more inclined to translate moral beliefs into practice with greater ease and are much more literal in following through on what they say they believe than their parents are.

Rather than being an immoral generation, young adults may well be just the opposite. There is much evidence in the way they insist upon reform in our social structures to suggest that they are really new moralists. Michael Harrington in a newspaper interview is reported to have said: "Far from being immoral or amoral, these kids drive you crazy talking about morality."

From the empirical data available two generalizations about the moral situation of young adults are possible. The first is that *a shift in morality is taking place in our society.* A liberalizing trend is clearly discernible, particularly among young adults. The Protestant ethic is declining in influence and is being replaced by what is described as a humanistic ethic. Such an ethic is emerging more from

[27] Quoted in *ibid.*, p. 599.

the influence of the behavioral sciences than from historical religion.

Philip E. Jacob, more than a decade ago, studied the values of college students and discovered that in spite of the moral conventionality of a majority a growing number were embracing secular and humanistic values.

> Against the background of earlier generations, these values of today's students look different. The undergirding of the Puritan heritage on which the major value assumptions of American society have rested is inconspicuous, if it is present at all. Perhaps these students are the forerunners of a major cultural and ethical revolution, the unconscious ushers of an essentially secular (though nominally religious), self-oriented (though group-conforming) society.[28]

Few young adults acknowledge that religion is an influence in moral decisions. Instead, moral practices tend to be pragmatic (solutions that are workable) and humanistic (a basic concern for the welfare of men). What seems to be basically reflected in the young adult generation is a movement from structured morality (prescribed moral rules) to expressive morality (conduct derived from the moral situation and the needs of persons).

Flacks provides us with a delineation of values inherent in a wide cross section of young adults and their parents. Some of these are: (1) individual development and self-expression, including the uninhibited and spontaneous response to the world; (2) free and noncalculated expressions of goodness instead of a morality of fixed rules; (3)

---

[28] Philip E. Jacob, *Changing Values in College* (New York: Harper & Row, 1957), p. 4.

appreciation of the beautiful with feeling and emotion; (4) creativity, including the liberation of expression; (5) authenticity or the realization of personal potentiality for oneself as well as others; (6) intimacy or the primacy of the I-Thou relation; and (7) compassion and sympathy for the suffering of others.[29]

The second generalization is that the *emerging morality is neither as new or as radical* as its proponents claim. One of our classical sociologists, William Graham Summer, has written that the moment society questions its own mores the mores will begin to lose their authority. If this be true, then the decline of the old morality began at the turn of the century with the rise of the psychological and social sciences. Although many young adults are not old enough to realize it, the religious sanctions upon which traditional morality was dependent have been under attack for half a century. In fact, probably the greatest period of moral upheaval in our society was between World War I and the depression of the 1930's. Victorianism collapsed in the face of urbanization, industrialization, woman suffrage, and a host of other developments. It was following World War II that the parents of our present young adults realized fully the fruits of a liberalization that had been forming for almost half a century.

What is different today is that we have systematic formulations of the humanistic ethic and there is a greater readiness to embrace it on the part of both adults and young adults. Sociologist Bennett M. Berger suggests that in spite of his desire to say that there is a new morality he cannot really support such a conclusion. He seems to think that

[29] Flacks, "Student Activists: Result, Not Revolt," pp. 21-23.

many of the values young adults articulate as new are really rooted in earlier moral skirmishes. What Berger does find new today is that there are more young adults in the population and this means there are more people to reject the older moralities and to embrace the newer ones.[30] Actually the moral conflict within our society has been overstated by many social critics. Simmons and Winograd are among those who have argued that young adults are deeply in conflict with their families over moral issues.[31] My own position is more closely aligned to Flacks' which sees a basic consistency between moral beliefs and practices of young adults and their parents.[32]

Our point can be illustrated by looking at that one moral issue that is always associated with young adulthood— sexual relationships between unmarried men and women. The popular interpretation of the situation is that young adults are becoming more promiscuous. But such a generalization is not supported by empirical research. Young adults today actually seem to be more restrained and less licentious in regard to sex. This does not mean that they are any less preoccupied with sex. What it does suggest is that the emotional context for sexual activities has changed considerably. Sex is now more open—more talked about— and greater pleasure and meaning are anticipated. Young adults are not engaging in sex more than previous generations did, but they are apparently enjoying it much more.

[30] Bennett M. Berger, "Hippie Morality—More Old Than New," *Trans-Action*, December, 1967, pp. 19-27.

[31] J. I. Simmons and Barry Winograd, *It's Happening* (Santa Barbara, Calif.: Marc-Laid Publications, 1966).

[32] Flacks, "Student Activists: Result, Not Revolt."

The revolution in sexual relations is in attitude and not in practice.

The major changes in sexual relations between men and women took place between 1910 and 1930. During this period the rate of premarital sexual intercourse increased three or four times, particularly among women. Since 1930 the number entering marriage as nonvirgins has increased slightly to approximately 50 percent, with the number of women engaging in premarital sex becoming about equal with the number of men.

There have been two significant trends developing since World War II that have become established facts with this new generation of young adults. The first is the decline of promiscuity, that is, sexual contact with more than one partner. Prior to World War II and especially prior to 1930 there were fewer women engaging in premarital intercourse, but with those who did it was with more than one partner. Today, at least half of the nonvirgins have slept only with the man they were going to marry. The second is that premarital intercourse usually takes place today within a meaningful relationship and between persons who intend to marry. For women particularly the first experience in sexual relations is associated with love and is a pleasurable event. In our society it is clear that sex today is less casual and more associated with commitment and marriage than in previous generations. We should not be misled by the outspoken advocates of various forms of free sexual associations. To a large extent they are ignored by young adults. The bulk of sexual intercourse continues to be oriented *toward* marriage. It seems clear that the female is actually less exploited than in the past and she is no longer viewed primarily as a sex object by herself and the male. Sex is experienced today within the context of human relations in which both partners are held as human beings with needs, expectations, and rights.

There is little doubt as to the direction young adults are going in formulating a morality of sexual conduct. The distance between the sexes is decreasing, and there is emerging greater sexual equality. In all probability the importance of sex will decrease in the foreseeable future as there is evidence that young adults are even less compulsive and less occupied with sex than their parents were. Sex is coming to be accepted as one of the natural experiences of life, not the dominant force in the man-woman relation. Sexual relations will increasingly become associated with affection and meaningful relationships.

For many young people the sexual pattern which they will choose will involve permissiveness with affection rather than waiting for marriage itself. The norm will become less formal or institutional and more expressive and humanistic. Robert Bell has summed up the situation this way.

> We have argued that the direct influence of religious institutions has been greatly weakened in this area, and there is no present evidence that religion is moving back as a major force over the premarital sexual values and behavior of the young. On the most general level, the movement in the American society seems to be toward greater sexual freedom.[33]

[33] *Premarital Sex in a Changing Society* (Englewood Cliffs, N. J.: Prentice-Hall, 1966), p. 172. Cf. Ira L. Reiss, *The Social Context of Premarital Sexual Permissiveness* (New York: Holt, Rinehart & Winston, 1968) and Mervin B. Freedman, *The College Experience* (San Francisco: Jossey-Bass, 1967), chapters 7 and 8.

The moral attitude of young adults is largely reflected in a student commission on social affairs established by the president of an important women's college in the west. The report called for more mutuality between administration, faculty, and students in the establishment of policy for student conduct and for students to be treated as adults with fewer rules regarding their private lives. Not only did students want to leave most moral behavior to the self-determination of individual students, but they also felt that the norm of such behavior was not moral codes or religious standards. The norm proposed was clearly a humanistic one, based on the extent to which behavior contributed to the actualization of the individual.

After a thoroughgoing study of sexual attitudes of the girls enrolled in the college and of the attitudes of a comparative sample at two neighboring men's colleges, the report made the following conclusions. (1) Few, if any, girls condemn (although not all would condone) sexual intimacy between couples who were serious about each other. (2) The girls were generaly unsure about the standards derived from their parents as they have not had an opportunity to fully test them. (3) A large percentage of the girls would not rule out the possibility of sexual intercourse with a young man they loved. (4) The majority derived their personal standards from parents and not from Christian ethics. Religion had little influence on their moral conduct. (5) The vast majority believed that morality today is an individual matter and that uniform standards cannot be applied to today's young adults. (6) The students did not condone a free expression of sex, although they were divided as to what is the most appropriate time for sexual expression. A few felt that it should be reserved for marriage, although a majority indicated that sex is most appropriate when associated with love, regardless of whether a formal marriage exists. They were all in agreement that sexual relations are representative of something larger than sex itself and that the formal line of right or wrong is not easily discerned.

What is represented here is a humanistic approach to human conduct with an emphasis upon flexibility and individual determination. That such a trend has been established in our society is not debatable; the issue does remain as to the ethical value of such a trend for the future of mankind.

Authority

The loss of authority may yet become the major issue of the present young adult generation. This is evidenced by two attitudes that have become widespread among young adults. The first is their disdain for the "God-given" and "American-given" traditions that have been foundational to our way of life. The second is that young adults, possibly for the first time in history, are challenging the legitimacy of adult authority.

This situation is in part due to the decline of supernatural religion with its emphasis upon the divine character of authority. For many young adults, moral conduct is good, not because it has a basis in metaphysics, but because it is workable and has proved useful through experience. Similarly, an adult deserves respect, not because he holds a position of authority, but because he as an individual has demonstrated his worth as a person and his competence in his position.

Almost all observers of the youth and young adult culture agree that in their eyes the adult empire with its institutions has fallen. Young adults are more aware than any previous generation of the inconsistencies of adults, the insincerity that has characterized much of their public performance, and the sheer inability of adult leaders to deal creatively with the problems of the age. With the loss of respect has come the downfall of authority.

Society should have anticipated young adult criticalness toward the formal structures of authority. They had been encouraged by their Protestant-like culture to question all authority, to think for themselves, and to exercise their personal consciences. Even more subversive has been the atmosphere of higher education that has touched approximately half of the young adult generation. Academic freedom has made it possible to bring together all manner of thinking, and young adults have been encouraged to make comparisons and to select that which was most meaningful. Even more important, the educational process no longer serves to indoctrinate the young but to stimulate critical thinking. Young adults are encouraged to be social critics, to evaluate their leaders, and to question the validity of their traditions. Experimental education has shifted the basis of authority from tradition to empiricism and pragmatism.

Quite possibly the issue is not really the loss of authority as some social critics have suggested. Instead the basis for authority is shifting in our society, and young adults, who are more or less unconsciously caught in the shift, are the first to reflect change.

Authority seems to be shifting from hierarchical structures to the democratic processes of shared responsibility according to people's ability and competence. The basis for authority lies not in the sacred or the traditional, but in the workable and the demands of a given situation. Although Carl Rogers may be overstating his case, he does reflect the humanistic basis for authority that is more far reaching than we have generally recognized. He writes, "Neither the Bible nor the prophets—neither Freud nor research—neither the revelation of God nor man—can take precedence over my own direct experience." [34]

The pitfall of the contemporary attitude is a lack of tradition or sense of history to validate present experience. In the crumbling of traditional authority, be it in the exercising of power or in moral conduct, the possibility that anarchic individualism will result is very real. There are signs in some quarters of the young adult culture that freedom is being defined in absolute terms.

In final reality the exercise of personal conscience and the creation of more flexible social structures will require a new kind of man with mature understanding of the breadth of tradition and a willingness to assume responsibility beyond the destruction of the old. In the long run this probably will require a larger understanding of history and a greater sensitivity to the whole of society than young adults have as yet demonstrated.

[34] *On Becoming a Person* (Boston: Houghton Mifflin, 1961), p. 24.

4

A Time in Life

Authorities generally agree that there is a sequence in the human life cycle called young or early adulthood. There is still much confusion as to the exact nature of this time in life, although recent students of human development have increasingly agreed that changes in the human organism continue to occur beyond the youth years and that there are particular developments that mark the years between seventeen or eighteen and the middle to late twenties. These are the years in which persons are deeply involved in a socio-psychological transition from adolescence to adulthood.

There have been few significant studies of the young adult sequence of the life cycle. The major exceptions have been the developmental tasks of early adulthood outlined by Robert Havighurst, the developmental needs of late adolescence described by Harry Stack Sullivan, the growth processes in young adulthood researched by R. H. White, the psycho-social crises of young adults formulated by Erik H. Erikson, and the more recent psychological studies of college students reported by Nevitt Sanford and Mervin B. Freedman.[1]

There are at least two reasons for this neglect. The first is that the age category of "young adulthood" simply did not exist until the second quarter of this century. There was almost no discussion of young or early adulthood in the literature on human development or personality theory until the 1950's. To a large extent, the years prior to adult maturity were viewed as an extension of adolescence and were labeled as the "older youth" years. As we indicated earlier, the growing complexity of urban life and the increased sophistication of the social and personality science have contributed to a greater specificity of age groups. In simpler societies the steps from adolescence to adulthood were carefully prescribed and easily assumed. For example, in rural America one became an adult by taking one's place on the family farm, getting married, and building a house. Since the way was carefully prescribed by society, there was little need for a period of testing and for trying out alternatives to adult life.

The second reason for neglecting the years beyond adolescence is that developmental psychologists placed major

[1] Robert J. Havighurst, *Developmental Tasks and Education* (London: Longmans, Green and Co., 1952); Harry Stack Sullivan, *The Interpersonal Theory of Psychiatry* (New York: W. W. Norton, 1953); R. W. White, *Lives in Progress* (New York: Dryden Press, 1952); Erik H. Erikson, *Young Man Luther* (New York: W. W. Norton, 1958) and *Identity: Youth and Crisis* (New York: W. W. Norton, 1968); Nevitt Sanford, *Self and Society* (New York: Atherton Press, 1966); and Mervin B. Freedman, *The College Experience* (San Francisco: Jossey-Bass, 1967).

importance upon infancy and childhood in the development of human personality. There has been almost a universal belief among Freudian and behaviorist theorists that the personality was fairly well shaped before the end of adolescence. Explaining why there have been so few young adult studies, Nevitt Sanford writes: "The prevailing opinion has been that the personality is pretty well formed or set by the age 18, and that what happens after that is to be understood mainly as expression of dispositions that have been established earlier, usually much earlier." [2]

Freedman, a co-researcher with Sanford, believes that the years between adolescence and adulthood are marked not only with significant needs but with important and far-reaching changes. Interestingly enough, the students in the Freedman-Sanford sample did not generally believe that they were in a time in life in which further development was possible.[3] It is likely that this reflects the prevailing attitude of society that young adulthood is not a significant era in the life of a person.

Although much of what we know about the distinctiveness of the young adult time in life has come from clinical studies (Erikson and Sullivan), the work of Freedman and Sanford is based upon empirical research of college age young people over a period of years. Some of their findings are:

1. Persons of this age are generally working on problems related to the stabilization of sex identity, the learning of sex roles, and the achievement of psychological intimacy.

[2] A special issue on "Personality Development During the College Years," *The Journal of Social Issues*, XII, 1956, 61.
[3] Freedman, *The College Experience*, p. 26.

2. During the young adult years, there is widespread increase in what Freedman describes as "rebellious independence." Persons tend to become more critical of authority (including parents, the state, and organized religion), more unconventional and nonconforming, more rejecting of traditional identity roles, less compulsive and more flexible and tolerant, and much more realistic.

3. At least among college age persons, there is an early phase in which persons are moving from an authoritarian orientation to a more sophisticated, complex, relative outlook on reality.

4. Finally, the studies discovered that young adults tend to become much more expressive in human relationships, especially in regard to sex. They are also much more in search of excitement and have increased openness to change and new experiences.[4]

As we will see later, these marks of the young adult years are inherent in the developing organism and are manifested in many of the problems and issues which are more characteristic of young adults than any other age group.

Problem of Definition

There are few cultures where growing up is as complex and stressful as it is presently in the United States. The maturing processes are generally universal although there is a wide difference in how the processes are manifest and resolved. Biological needs are more or less similar in all human societies. How these needs are met is culturally defined and varies from society to society.

[4] *Ibid.*, pp. 27-31; also Sanford, *Self and Society*, pp. 52 ff., 274 ff.

It is generally agreed that non-Western cultures are more relaxed in regard to growing up, having but a few simple guideposts marking the entrance to adulthood. In less complex societies, as well as in historical or tradition-oriented groups, initiatory rites are usually the mark of passage from childhood to adulthood. Such rites are generally family oriented and serve to legitimatize sexual expressions and to invest in the new adult the authority of adulthood. Developmental stages for extended youth and young adult age groups are either nonexistent or not very dramatic in their manifestations. Preindustrial societies tend to move individuals quite early into adult responsibility; that is, just as soon as they are able to master the required tests for passage into the adult community. In industrial societies such as existed in most of the Western nations prior to World War II, youth were dependent upon their parents much longer—often into the twenties—and passage into the adult community required the attainment of a level of maturity, experience, and demonstrated competence. With the rise of the newer technical societies, such as the United States, appreciation for elders diminished as young people ignored traditional routes to adulthood and entered openly into struggles to wrench new power away from adults.

As societies have become more complex, the family has ceased to be the basic unit of socialization. Increasingly the function of initiating youth into adulthood has passed from the parents and the other elders of the family into the hands of peer-group institutions established to educate and prepare persons for the assumption of adult responsibility. Since most of these newer social institutions have limited functions and are geared to specific age groups, the segregation of generations has resulted, and the age group subcultures have intensified. This has resulted in a growing struggle for power between the initiates and the established adults.[5]

Historically, it has been basic to most societies for a person to pass into adulthood after he has met three criteria: (1) he has demonstrated that he has been educated and trained according to the expectations of the community, including a thorough indoctrination in the heritage of the society; (2) he has proved himself capable of defending the community and performing a trade or vocation; and (3) he has given evidence of his adulthood by successfully mating with the opposite sex. Rites of passage symbolize these accomplishments and mark the end of adult control and the assumption of adult life.[6]

Probably the most important study of how societies structure age groups and care for the generational problems is S. N. Eisenstadt's *From Generation to Generation*. From his study of both primitive and modern societies he concludes that one of the basic criteria for adulthood in all societies is the establishment of legitimate sexual relations. By this he means not only engaging in sexual intercourse but establishing a family as well.[7] The sexual expression is so fundamental in some societies that young people are encouraged to demonstrate their approaching adulthood by engaging in sexual intercourse, and in some places the

[5] The relationship between social change and the rise of new age-group subcultures has been made by James S. Coleman, *The Adolescent Society* (New York: The Free Press, 1961), chap. 1.

[6] S. N. Eisenstadt, "Archtypal Patterns of Youth," *Daedalus*, Winter, 1962, pp. 31-32.

[7] See pp. 30 f.

young woman is required to successfully become pregnant. It may not be too absurd to suggest that even in our contemporary situation young adults unofficially tend to prove their adult status by various forms of sexual activities. There is no doubt that both men and women are under some social compulsion to prove that they have achieved adulthood by acting sexually. In fact, psychologists feel that some girls become pregnant prior to marriage intentionally in order to establish themselves in a new peer group.

The human organism in the less organized societies is much freer to grow up with limited restrictions and to let human needs dictate the forms in which human development will take. This is in contrast to middle-class Protestant cultures where expectations are often carefully prescribed and are often in conflict with basic biological drives and psychological needs. As these rigid expectations begin to break down in a more technical and increasingly urban society, the way to maturity is often an uncharted maze and is at times either very confusing or filled with various contradictions. Not only are the traditional rites signifying entrance into adulthood being abandoned by contemporary societies, but the symbols marking the beginning of adulthood are no longer universally applicable. Completing the education, getting started in a vocation, and establishing sexual relations no longer come in a planned sequence or have any relationship to one's age, maturity, or readiness to assume adult responsibility. In fact, today the establishment of sexual relations often comes before the completion of education or the beginning of adult employment.

Today young adulthood is placed more within historical

events than chronological age. Some boys find themselves in armed combat in a foreign land before they are out of their teens, and many girls find themselves married before they complete high school. The rapidly changing events of our present age often hasten some adult commitments and delay others indefinitely.

There is evidence that we are no more clear as to the social function or purpose of young adulthood than of adolescence. With the old generational structures disappearing we seem to vacillate between understanding adolescents as "big" children or as "little" adults. The adolescent is caught, on one hand, with restrictions representing immaturity such as early evening curfew laws and, on the other hand, with commandments to grow up, take responsibility, and be serious about life. Similarly young adults are viewed at one time as older youth and at another time as younger adults. As a result there is little integrity in the young adult developmental sequence and no clear passage into the adult generation. This tends to reinforce a peer group subculture and to force persons to linger in young adulthood longer than is really necessary. Young adults do not find it worthwhile to go on to adulthood and therefore choose to remain permanently on the threshold of maturity.

As Edgar Z. Friedenberg suggests, a culture's use of language is a precise clue as to what is taking place. Our present dilemma in regard to the years between eighteen and thirty is revealed in our inability to describe what these years signify in the life cycle. One needs only to survey both the popular and professional literature to discover that persons in their late teens and twenties are referred to as young people, older youth, late adolescents, early adults, young adults, postadolescents, and preadults. In fact, it has been necessary for us to perpetuate the confusion here because of our reliance upon the research of others who have not been consistent as to whom they are really describing. Even as notable an authority as Erikson is not precise in his use of language and appears to talk about youth, adolescents, and young adults as if they were similar phenomenon.

Legally adulthood begins with the statutory age of responsibility which ranges from fifteen to twenty-one years of age, depending upon local laws. Ironically state and national laws are contradictory. Some states hold youth criminally responsible at sixteen, others at seventeen or eighteen; financial responsibility is fixed generally between eighteen and twenty-one; and social responsibility (night curfew limitation) is set at eighteen in many cities. On the other hand, the national government considers a youth old enough for compulsive military service at eighteen. But many states feel that the same youth should not marry without parental permission or vote before he is twenty-one.

The confusion, in part at least, is related to the nature of the maturing processes, particularly in those developmental sequences between older childhood and adulthood. Not only are profound physical changes occurring in adolescence, but the personality of young adults is coming to terms with deep and significant drives and urges, and the individual is having to make decisions that will set the course of his adult life.

The several sequences of childhood tend to slide into each other, and this is equally true of adolescence, young adulthood, and adulthood. There are no clear-cut lines marking the end of one sequence and the beginning of another. In spite of this some persons have acted as if there were arbitrary lines staking out the age periods. Such a concept of human development is contrary to the nature of the human personality. One just does not get up on a particular morning, consult a chart, and declare "Today, I am an adult."

Developmental Tasks

One of the ways for understanding human growth processes is to see that there are a series of age periods, each containing a series of prescribed tasks to be learned before an individual is ready for the next stage in his development. Havighurst, a leading theorist of human development, has been the prime influence in the formulation of this developmental task concept. One of the earliest to describe an age group between adolescence and adulthood, he believes that early adulthood is a time in which some of the most important decisions of life are made.

Developmental tasks emerge out of the maturation needs of an individual and the societal demands on him. In contrast to Erikson who centers upon the inside crises of human development, Havighurst emphasizes the outside demands which an individual must meet before he is ready to move ahead in the human life cycle. His emphasis results in the age periods developing a set of ritualistic demands which must be learned—in the manner designated by society—in order for the young adult to grow up. An example of this is the social pressure upon young adults, and particularly young women, to marry before their mid-twenties. Those who choose to delay marriage or to avoid it all together are looked upon by society as being either social failures, or oddballs, or sometimes both.

The conforming nature of the developmental tasks is reflected in the following definition provided by Havighurst:

> A developmental task is a task which arises at or about a certain period in the life of the individual, successful achievement of which leads to his happiness and to success with later tasks, while failure leads to unhappiness in the individual, disapproval by the society, and difficulty with later tasks.[8]

Havighurst's scheme tends to establish clear-cut age periods in which there are a series of socially determined requirements for each stage to be met by the individual at the time and in ways prescribed by society. Deviation is usually discouraged and generally leads to social disapproval. Havighurst does acknowledge that there are individual differences, and this is particularly true in the egocentric nature of early adulthood; but at the same time the weight of the tasks are in the direction of universal conformity to social demands. The result is that Havighurst's developmental tasks tend to be oriented to a particular historical period and are largely culturally bound to middle-class values and the "normal" rather than the exceptional.

In all fairness to Havighurst's important contribution to our understanding of young adults, it should be pointed out that he has more recently acknowledged that the complexity of modern society makes a strong case for more variety in

[8] *Developmental Tasks and Education*, p. 2.

the ways that individuals choose to meet the tasks of human development.[9]

In his classic discussion of early adulthood Havighurst indicates that this age period begins at eighteen and ends at thirty. Included in the stage are eight developmental tasks which young adults must learn on their way to middle adulthood. They are: (1) selecting a mate, (2) learning to live with a marriage partner, (3) starting a family, (4) rearing children, (5) managing a home, (6) getting started in an occupation, (7) taking on civic responsibility, and (8) finding a congenial social group.

Organismic View of Maturing

In order to get away from the pitfalls of a single explanation for what takes place as one moves from adolescence to adulthood, recent students of human development have attempted to look at the process of maturing from a multidimensional context. Just as Havighurst concentrated upon social traits, others have focused on other single explanations, such as psychological needs, biological forces, sexual manifestations, and cultural rites and rituals. Although each of these viewpoints is useful and worthwhile, none adequately explains all the factors which are at work when an individual is growing up. It was Harvard University's Henry A. Murray who pioneered in interdisciplinary studies of personality because he believed that "living beings must be studied as living wholes."

An organismic or wholistic view of human development

[9] *The Educational Mission of the Church* (Philadelphia: Westminster Press, 1965), p. 47.

has been applied to the study of young adults by Douglas Heath, professor of psychology at Haverford College. For more than twenty years he has been involved in longitudinal studies of college students and the problems of maturing. He has concluded that the "maturing person can be understood in terms of five interrelated developmental dimensions." [10] The five dimensions are always present from childhood to old age, although they become increasingly present as the individual moves toward adulthood. In a real sense, what Heath is saying is that each of these five dimensions represents a different way of conceptualizing the whole or basic growth process.

1. The first of these five dimensions is a movement *toward stability*. Stability is integrating the polarities of openness and centering down. The movement toward stability is from an ever-shifting personal existence to a greater constancy in self-image, intellectual skills, values, and interpersonal relations.

2. Maturity is secondly understood as a movement *toward integration*. This suggests that a person is not only achieving greater unity in his outlook on life, but is also increasingly able to incorporate his ideas, values, and friendship patterns into his total personality.

3. A movement *toward allocentricism* is still another dimension of maturing. As Heath writes, "The thrust of development is from autocentricism, egocentricism and narcissism, from impulsive domination by one's own needs,

[10] "Maturing and the Liberal Education Tradition," an unpublished paper reporting research in process, p. 5. Much of the material in this section is the result of an extended discussion with Dr. Heath. See also his work *Explorations of Maturity* (New York: Appleton-Century-Crofts, 1965).

toward the gradual incorporation into the self of that which originally belonged outside of one's body." [11] It is the ability to incorporate into one's personality the needs of others and assume some responsibility for their welfare.

4. A maturing person is moving in a fourth dimension *toward autonomy*. This is similar to Erikson's concept of ego integrity—one's ability to be flexible when need be and at the same time to achieve the strength and courage to maintain oneself in the face of opposition and social pressures. It is to live with conviction out of the values and intellectual understanding which one possesses and at the same time to be open to the possibility that one may be wrong and may need to have a change of mind.

5. Finally, maturity requires an ever-increasing ability to *symbolize one's experiences* in some meaningful way. Heath believes that with increased maturity comes also the ability to transcend experience and to reflect and interpret its significance.

A Configuration Model

Another way of understanding young adult development is to view the growing person as a life-system related to a configuration or a field of influences and forces.

Human development is a dynamic process in which there is a configuration or pattern of social systems and cultural forces interacting to form an ever-changing self-system or life-system. By choosing a configuration model, it becomes possible for us to understand young adulthood as a developmental sequence within the total life cycle. In addition,

[11] "Maturing and the Liberal Education Tradition," p. 11.

it is possible to view the young adult in several contexts—psychologically, sociologically, culturally, etc.—and at the same time remain aware that other contexts are also present and are having influence upon the life-system. In fact, one of the problems in most popular interpretations of young adult culture is that generalizations are made from looking at the most visible young adults from one point of view. It is our purpose here to establish a model of development which will allow broader perspectives upon the changes characteristic of young adulthood.

It is here proposed that young adulthood can more accurately be understood when viewed as a configuration of biological needs, social forces, human interactions, psychological experiences, and cultural demands. By viewing the young adult developmental sequence as a dynamic set of experiences all located in a larger system of human relationships, we may hopefully avoid oversimplications, and clarification of the nature and purpose of this age group may possibly take place.

From our point of view the following definition of young adulthood can be formulated.

Young adulthood is a developmental sequence which ascends at a particular time in the life cycle as psychosocial crises of the personality system interact with social forces, cultural expectations, and other personal systems, resulting in the reshaping and expansion and further integration of the life-system of the individual and in the development and modification of culture.

In spite of the technicality of it the definition is functional in guiding us to an understanding of the variety of forms which young adult life can take as individuals not only move from adolescence to adulthood but interact with each other to form a young adult subculture, which in turn influences, and is influenced by, the larger culture. The definition provides us with several insights.

1. Young adulthood is a developmental sequence which ascends at a particular time in the growth of the human organism. A person cannot just decide he is a young adult because he feels like it—not even those who long to identify with the "think-young" generation. The developmental sequence of young adulthood arises at the time in which basic needs of the human organism interact with the expectations of society. Chronological age by itself is only a clue to young adulthood and can only approximate the time that the developmental sequence may be expected to begin and end. There is, however, a time plan to personality development represented by a sequence of experiences and crises marking the various phases of growth. Young adulthood does not just happen, it occurs when the human organism reaches a particular stage of development, and this stage in turn is recognized and acknowledged by society.

As Erikson has helped us to see, human growth consists of a ground plan in which all of the several "parts" are continuously present. For example, the sexual crisis of young adulthood is never absent from the human organism, even in infancy or old age, although it may not always be dominant in influence. At a special time in the development of the personality, one of the parts will ascend to dominance resulting in both a personal and a social crisis that must be resolved in order for further growth to successfully take place. With all the parts continuously active and inter-related, the one that has become dominant is influenced and formed by what has already taken place and by what can be expected.

In planned sequence each part, represented by a psycho-social stage, gives rise to a life crisis which must be resolved in the context of cultural demands. As each crisis of the human organism ascends and is resolved, it continues as an active force in the personality to be joined in time by other crises to create a functioning whole.[12]

This psychosocial plan of Erikson includes eight life stages of human development. Each life stage in turn emerges on top of the previous stage to form an expanding configuration of personality. The larger configuration of the life cycle includes a developing individual in his particular life stage of development, but also other individuals who are each in a particular life-stage. In this way the "life cycle is an integrated psychosocial phenomenon" in which one individual's life stages are "interliving, cogwheeling with the stages of others which moves him along as he moves them." [13] Young adulthood, therefore, can be understood as always being a part of a larger system "cogwheeling" with the other life stages of the life cycle. Such an insight into the young adult developmental sequence delivers us from older models with their emphasis upon "growth steps" or age-group categories. Furthermore, a configuration approach to personal development eliminates the tendency to segre-gate age groups narrowly for program purposes. Each de-

[12] Erik H. Erikson, *Identity and the Life Cycle* (New York: International Universities Press, 1959), p. 52.
[13] *Insight and Responsibility* (New York: W. W. Norton, 1964), p. 114.

velopmental sequence needs the others, and Erikson sees problems of psychological growth inherent in the tendency to cut one generation off from another. Actually, the sequence of time called young adulthood is socially relevant and functional only as it is understood in relation to the other development sequences. A fully functional person is required to see his life as a part of a larger plan with a purpose toward which he moves.

Recent talk of a generational gap may be exaggerated somewhat, although there is much evidence that a segment of youth and young adults with some adult support is disassociating itself from the generational cycle. Regardless of the advantages of such protests, and there are many from the point of view of reform, there are some distinct disadvantages psychologically. From a context of psychological growth, there is inherent in the human organism the need for young adults to sustain some sameness and continuity even in the process of forging a new life and culture.

The so-called hippie subculture, for example, has cut itself off from the generational cycle—not out of rebellion but because it is closed to change. To return to an agrarian style of existence more characteristic of the nineteenth century is to close oneself to the openness possible in an urban society. The radical left, on the other hand, has so opened itself to change that it has also been cut off from the generational cycle through its repudiation of any sameness. The psychological process of maturing requires not only an openness to the future represented by the growth process, but at the same time it also requires the preservation of sameness and some of the essential features of a stable society.

2. Young adulthood is marked by the rise of psychosocial crises which demand personal as well as cultural resolution. Crisis denotes a turning point in which there are positive and negative possibilities or alternatives. In each developmental sequence an individual is confronted with a crisis which has psychological and sociocultural ramifications. With positive and negative possibilities in each crisis, it does not become a matter of electing one and ignoring the other. The developing individual must experience and learn how to deal with the negative side of the crisis as well as realize satisfactory resolutions on the positive side. For example, the young adult cannot escape the experience of loneliness (isolation) and must learn along with belonging (intimacy) how to deal with the issues arising on both sides of this developmental crisis.

Erikson has reacted to the way his eight stages have been misused as an attainment scale. The tendency is to separate each crisis from the others and to lift up the need to accomplish only the positive aspect of each crisis, creating in effect a kind of outward program of achievement.

The psychosocial crisis which arises to dominance in the young adult developmental sequence is intimacy versus isolation. But present at the same time in the developmental sequence are all the earlier crises along with later ones yet to come to ascendency. The configuration of all the life crises and how they are experienced and resolved determines how the young adult will experience the intimacy crisis.[14]

[14] Cf. Erikson's *Young Man Luther* for an expanded and documented account of this view of young adulthood.

What the young adult crisis represents is the *possibility* of a person's intimacy or deeper engagement with others. At the same time, there is the possibility that one will experience isolation, primarily by excluding or repudiating those who offer the most possibility for intimacy. An example of isolation is disdainment for the opposite sex.

Intimacy is more than relationships with others. It is the losing and finding of oneself in another, especially in friendship, love, and sexual relations. Erikson writes, "Intimacy is really the ability to fuse your identity with somebody else's without fearing that you're going to lose something yourself." [15]

Active in the young adult development sequence in what Erikson calls "later forms" are the earlier life crises. Already active and itching for their special time of ascendency are the developmental crises of adulthood and mature age.

It might help us to understand better our configuration model of young adulthood if the life cycle could be understood as an upward, expanding spiral. The base of the spiral is a small circle containing in some form each of the developmental crises. The base of the spiral is infancy and its crisis of basic trust versus distrust. As the personality develops, expanding circles containing all the developmental crises in their resolved or unresolved state are added upward. The expanding circles include an ever-growing range of social experiences, cultural influences, and the need for integrating more fully all of the factors that make up the field of one's existence or life system. Young adulthood comes close to the top of the spiral indicating the emer-

[15] Richard I. Evans, *Dialogue with Erik Erikson* (New York: Harper & Row, 1967), p. 48.

116

gence of maturity: a more fully functioning and integrated personality.

The spiraling life cycle includes, therefore, the eight life stages of human development. Beginning with infancy and moving toward young adulthood and on beyond to mature age, these stages are: infancy, trust versus mistrust; early childhood, autonomy versus shame and doubt; play age, initiative versus guilt; school age, industry versus inferiority; adolescence, identity versus identity diffusion; *young adult*, intimacy versus isolation; adulthood, generativity versus self-absorption; and mature age, integrity versus disgust and despair.[16]

3. There is a cultural relativism to the young adult sequence of the life cycle. Transcultural studies have found that genetic or life crises along with the maturing processes seem to be universal; that is, they seem to be common to the human organism in a variety of societies and cultures. The way the crises are manifested—the manner in which they ascend, are met, and resolved—varies not only from culture to culture but also among classes and races. If such a conclusion is accepted, a cultural relativism must be included in our definition of young adult. There are universal needs that arise because young adults are human beings who experience in some way the particular developmental sequence associated with their time in life. The way in which the young adult developmental sequence is experienced and perceived will vary from person to person, depending upon the idiosyncrasies of each individual young adult, his life history, his place within the larger

[16] Erikson, *Identity and the Life Cycle*, pp. 120, 166.

culture (his subculture), and his patterns of social inter-action.

An understanding of the young adult developmental se-quence must always be balanced by clinical studies of in-dividual young adults on one hand and with anthropologi-cal studies of young adult culture on the other hand.

4. Social interaction and interpersonal relations play a significant role in the young adult developmental se-quence. Erikson has charted what he calls the "radius of significant relations." [17] As one might imagine, the radius of relations increases with age and experience. According to Erikson the range extends from the maternal person in in-fancy to mankind in general in mature age. For the young adult developmental sequence, the significant rela-tions are peer group; partners in friendship, love, and sex; and coworkers. In addition to these significant relations a configuration study of the young adult would include other significant persons, both in the past and in the present. The role of adults, especially parents, is an important factor in the developmental sequence. Especially significant are the interaction between the parent and child in the emotional weaning process and the reestablishment of new adult-to-adult relations.

An important study, neglected in most discussions of young adulthood, is contained in the work of Harry Stack Sullivan.[18] The interpersonal psychology of Sullivan is un-

[17] *Ibid.*, p. 166.

[18] *The Interpersonal Theory of Psychiatry.* See also Jane Pearce and Saul Newton, *The Conditions of Human Growth* (New York: Citadel Press, 1963) for a good introduction to Sullivan's concepts.

doubtedly influenced by George H. Mead's social psychology wherein the developing personality is conceived as a self-system arising out of significant social experiences. Present experiences are organized and hung on to by the previous self to form the expanding personality. Widening and deepening experiences are the marks of the maturing life. Young adulthood is a time of expanding relations and experiences and the enlargement of the self-system or what I prefer to call the life-system.

The clinical studies of Sullivan reinforce the significance of interpersonal relationships in the development of young adults. His point of view is that the individual personality is determined to a large extent by the quality of relationships that one has with other persons. As Lewis Sherrill suggests, individuals are formed, deformed, and reformed by their relationships.

Interpersonal relationships always occur within a social and cultural context which influences the value and meaning which individuals will give to them. But in spite of the content derived from social systems and culture, the personality remains always an independent system and never becomes merely a reflection of his relationships and social environment. The individual's relationship to his own organism and the uniqueness of his life experiences give distinctiveness to his personality. One's own awareness and perception influence the experiences he takes in upon himself and how he organizes these into his life-system. The individual *focuses in* on meaningful experiences and *focuses out* on anxiety-producing and nonmeaningful experiences.

119

5. The rise of lustful feelings is probably the dominant force in the young adult sequence of development. According to Sullivan, late adolescence and young adulthood are especially marked by the need to make achievements in interpersonal relationships which are sexual in nature. He describes this as the need to make lustful achievements.[19]

Biological maturation is not a particular characteristic of young adulthood as physical growth is near completion. What is *characteristic* is the rise of lustful or genital feelings which require adequate and satisfactory expression.

The young adult developmental sequence is a time when persons are working on interpersonal relations along three levels:

(1) The establishment of a "fully human or mature repertory of interpersonal relations." [20]

(2) The achievement of intimacy, which may be defined as collaboration with at least one other person.

(3) The satisfaction of lustful power, which Sullivan defines as "genital activity in pursuit of orgasm." [21]

Although society often attempts to deny it, the sexual nature of human development is never so powerful in human personality as in the young adult years. Sullivan's own clinical studies conclude that young adulthood is primarily a time of lust, meaning that the genital drive and the need for sexual expression are firmly felt. Sex becomes a

[19] *Ibid.*, pp. 297 ff.
[20] *Ibid.*, p. 297.
[21] *Ibid.*, p. 264.

dominant concern as young adults focus in on what they may like "in the way of genital behavior and how to fit it into the rest of life." [22]

6. *Young adulthood is not an end in itself, but a means toward an ongoing human process of maturing.* Maturity is not a static goal that one reaches at a certain age in life—such as the attainment of adulthood. Rather it is a dynamic process by which an individual grows in his capacity to work out unique integrations and styles of existing as a person, and to come to greater self-acceptance and continued self-expansion. The maturity young adults strive toward is always unfinished business.

It is in this regard that the "significant adult" becomes an important resource for the person in the young adult developmental sequence. As an individual reaches out for adulthood with all of its problems and potentialities, he has a need for someone who has been there to affirm that the future is worth achieving. Such affirmation cannot be paternalistic; instead it occurs within a context of mutual relations where the adult is permitted to remain adult and the young adult is free to remain what he actually is.

Functional Significance of Young Adulthood

Young adulthood should be allowed to be what it is. This developmental sequence is significant because it represents a time when normal but powerful human issues rise to ascendency to be met and resolved. Culture determines, in part, how these issues are resolved; although the young

[22] *Ibid.*, p. 297.

adult himself may create new culture forms by meeting the unique needs of his generation. When the latter occurs, young adulthood and the emerging cultural forms will almost always come in conflict with more established patterns, represented by more traditional forms. This process of interaction between the new and the old results in modification of each subculture and leads to new cultural norms. In times such as the present the rapidity by which cultural change occurs and the size of the young adult population involved contribute to what can be called a "culture gap." Young adults are creating new cultural forms more rapidly than they are accepting old forms, and the new is appearing faster than an older generation can integrate it. In this cultural interaction the older generation functions to stabilize society, and the new generation serves to ferment or impregnate society with newness.

There is still another function which young adulthood serves within society. It is an initiatory phase when persons pass from the immaturity of youth into the maturity of adulthood. Young adulthood can be understood functionally as a transitional era between youth and adulthood. It is a time when a person puts aside childish ways and establishes himself in more mature ways. Persons within the young adult developmental sequence are in a time of testing, of trying out various alternatives for life, and of formulating a life-system which gives meaning and significance to their lives. To be an adult is not really the goal; instead the goal is to emerge into new levels of maturity.

Another way of describing the nature of young adulthood is to say that it affords an opportunity for persons, at the right time within the life cycle, to go into "neutral" in order that the life-system can be opened up for testing and overhauling before it closes down with some basic commitments.

Society seems at times to be impatient and even intolerant of the transitional nature of young adulthood. On one hand, the young adult is told to "hurry up, grow up, settle down"; on the other hand, he is told "not to rush life, to take it easy, you're only a kid without experience."

In actuality only the rich and the poor are really free to experience a moratorium between youth and adulthood. The middle class, caught up in the symbols of success, is not free to keep opportunities for commitment open until life has been explored and tested. The hippie movement is providing a time to go into neutral for many young adults who are finding it helpful to drop out of society with its demands for commitments in order to examine some possible alternatives for life. The emerging style of bachelorhood, especially among young women, serves the same purpose. The military is performing a similar function, especially for those without the financial resources to travel and to experience the different.

Erikson sees great value in a transitional experience as he indicates: "The period can be viewed as a *psychosocial moratorium* during which the individual through free role experimentation may find a niche in some section of his society—a niche which is firmly defined and yet seems to be uniquely made for him." [23]

Before the transition is completed each young adult must achieve a sense of worth through creative and produc-

---

[23] *Identity and the Life Cycle*, p. 111.

tive efforts. Such an achievement is not always immediate and most naturally comes toward the close of the young adult developmental sequence. Responsibility emerges out of a life-system that has discovered its individuality and has experienced fully a life beyond itself. Only as he finds himself—and another—is the young adult ready to assume responsibility for the next generation.

5

From Adolescence to Adulthood

Young adulthood may best be understood as a time of transition from adolescence to adulthood. In a broad sense, of course, every age group represents something of a transitional experience as the very process of human development is that of moving from one stage in life to another. But young adulthood seems to be more pronounced as a transition than any other stage in the life cycle.

First of all, it is a major watershed of life, dividing children and youth from adulthood and marking the end of dependency and the beginning of independency. One of the major crises comes as young adults attempt to emancipate themselves from family controls. Such a break is never easy—especially from mother—and this is accentuated today because many young adults remain economically dependent in order to further their education while at the same time they attempt to break the apron strings.

In the second place, unlike those involved in the movement from childhood to adolescence, young adults are generally making their transition beyond the protection of the home environment. After graduation from high school most young adults leave home and soon find themselves free from old certainties and social patterns. This results in something of a psychosocial state of neutrality that often appears to adults as a kind of irresponsible aimlessness. In actuality, young adulthood is another latency period in the life cycle, permitting persons to hover for a time before assuming the responsibilities of adulthood. It is a twilight zone in which persons can experiment with forms of adult life before setting down to new commitments and patterns of life.[1]

A third distinction is that during these transitional years young adults are making the decisions that will basically form the future course of their adult life. Ross Snyder prefers to understand young adulthood as an era—a time of significant happenings—rather than just a latency period.[2] And in some regards he is right because there is inherent in the young adult situation basic questions to be resolved. Young adults are not only struggling to find themselves as persons, but are also trying to make decisions about work and marriage—the two fundamental expressions of human life.

Finally, young adulthood is loaded with the possibilities for failure. Many experience, in varying degree, personal and social breakdown during these years. If statistics of

[1] Erikson, *Identity: Youth and Crisis*, pp. 156 f.
[2] Ross Snyder, ed., *The Young Adult*, a special issue of *The Chicago Theological Seminary Register*, November, 1959, p. 11.

social pathologies are any indication, then young adulthood is a time of great stress and strain. In almost every kind of social disorganization, the young adult age group appears to be preponderant. Even among so-called normal young adults, the process of becoming adult is for most a disillusioning experience.[3]

As we indicated in the previous chapter, the substance for the young adult time in life is a cluster of crises which must be resolved if one is to move with any semblance of adequacy into adulthood. Although the stimuli for the crises are intrinsic to the organism, the shape the crises take and how they are resolved is influenced by the culture in which an individual lives.

Each crisis not only requires a fundamental decision, but has within that decision the potentiality for further growth and fulfillment as well as the possibility for regression and deformity. Erikson understands these crises in development as "turning points" or as crucial periods of "increased vulnerability and heightened potential, and therefore the ontogenetic source of generational strength and maladjustment." [4]

It seems clear that the years between youth and adulthood are fundamental in laying the groundwork for living successfully as an adult. Far from being a phase for sowing wild oats or for getting kicks young adulthood is a crucial time in life, a time for making basic decisions and choosing the kind of an adult one is to become. These are the years in which the basis for either an authentic life or a dis-

---

[3] Percival M. Symonds and Arthur R. Jensen, *From Adolescent to Adult* (New York: Columbia University Press, 1961), p. 199.

[4] Erikson, *Identity: Youth and Crisis*, p. 92.

honest one is established. We shall now turn to a discussion of the developmental crises which seem to be most inherent in the process of becoming adult.

Self-Definition

A crisis which arises in adolescence and carries over with great force into young adulthood is that of *self-definition versus personal vagueness*. It involves the psychosocial task of finding an identity or a self-image which will bring into an integrated whole the various roles and expectations of adult life. As one young woman put it, "I am living the life of three people, and I cannot get them to fit together." By this she meant she was expected to be a child who is obedient to and dependent on a parent; a secretary who is mature, efficient, and independent; and a bachelor girl who is sexually attractive, responsive in male-female relations, and a potential wife. Self-definition for her and for most young adults involves selecting out of a fragmented collection of expectations, relationships, and ideals those which are most meaningful and putting them together into an integrated definition for life. In short, self-definition is deciding what one wants to become as well as what one does not want to be.

A danger is that a definition for life will come too quickly or will come by default because of circumstances. A premarital pregnancy, for example, may force an individual into the role of a parent and even possibly that of a wife before she has an opportunity to try out a definition of herself as a career woman. She and others like her may wake up in middle life to discover that they have a job, a mate, and a way of life which they detest. Presently, there are a large number of middle-aged adults who are shifting careers or who are dissolving their marriages because as young adults they made hasty or premature decisions which have proved incompatible with their basic identities. Society has been largely responsible for this because of its unwillingness to recognize the *waiting* that young adulthood requires. As one young person puts it, "We are having to struggle to keep from getting our personality too soon."

As we have already indicated, a psychosocial moratorium functions to keep the personality open long enough for the young adult to experiment with or try out various modes of being adult. Only after an individual has tested the options open to him is he ready to take his place in society as a mature and responsible adult. With the resolution of the crisis of self-definition the moratorium ends, and the person is ready to settle down to a situation which seems to be made uniquely for him.

To find one's identity for life involves what classical theology describes as "calling" or "vocation." Vocation has to do with locating oneself uniquely within history and finding a purpose that transcends egotistical desires and needs. Self-definition requires a cause or worthwhile purpose to which a person can give himself unreservedly. To fail to find this larger purpose for life may leave an individual unconfirmed as to the worth of his identity and may result in a vague kind of self-indulgence under the guise of some sort of purpose. One readily perceives this in the mother who claims she is living for her children when actually she is using them to massage her own undefined identity.

The search for self-definition is one of the causes of the present unrest among young adults. With the exception of the Peace Corps, designed by the late President Kennedy, society has been impoverished for young adult causes. The most society could offer young adults were pale reflections of a bygone age such as Americanism, a nonsensical war in Asia, and first aid for a crumbling religious order. As a natural response young adults developed styles of protest and dissent and formulated causes opposing the old order, with its racism, educational bureaucracy, and militarism. The young adult unrest cannot finally be understood until society can appreciate the problem of identity which this generation is experiencing.[5]

It is a bit frightening to know that it is in such times of rapid social change, when there is a demise of leaders and worthwhile goals, that the "Hitlers" have the greatest appeal to youth. When there is great diffusion of personality as well as ideology in a society, the young will sometimes take a shortcut and take on a ready-made identity, either one provided by a demagogue or one mass-produced by Madison Avenue.

There is much evidence that young adults today are having difficulty finding themselves. Because they have not found an identity, they are not only delayed in their development but are caught in a kind of personal vagueness. This is of course not new with this generation, as many of their parents are passing through middle age without the slightest notion as to who they are. Willie Loman in

[5] Cf. *Ibid.*, pp. 15-43.

Arthur Miller's *Death of a Salesman* is representative of the frustrated adults who have never gotten hold of life and have had to resort to an artificial personality as a cover-up.

Part of the personality diffusion among the young is naturally the result of the confusion about life which besets the adult generation. The middle-class family particularly has failed to provide clear models of adulthood or to give the young adult the support he needs as he searches for his own model. As Sullivan has demonstrated in his clinical studies, a healthy self-image requires positive social images. He means by this that we become to a large extent what other people tell us we are. This does not mean that personality is solely a reflection of others, although the definition we achieve for ourselves does need confirmation by persons who are especially close to us.[6] This is what Erikson calls the double task of identity formation.[7] The young adult not only needs to define himself, but he also needs to be defined by others.

The young adult struggles with the question of "who am I?" along with the question of "who do you say I am?" and he must find a correlation between the answers he gets from the two questions. Conflicting answers add to the diffusion and vagueness which he is already experiencing. When significant persons in the configuration of relations fail to offer identification when needed, the young adult turns either to mass personification of adulthood or produces an exaggeration of an identity. The playboy look is

[6] Sullivan, *The Interpersonal Theory of Psychiatry*, especially pp. 246, 300 ff.
[7] *Insight and Responsibility*, pp. 90 ff.

an example of the former and the hippie is representative of the latter.

The frustration for all too many young adults in our society is that they not only fail to get the confirmation which they need, but they get instead negative images of unworth. On one hand, they struggle to say "I am"; on the other hand, they are being told by the adult culture "You are NOT!" Such a psychological negation is enhanced by the depersonalization which has not as yet been controlled by large segments of our society. This is nowhere more true than in the social institutions which are designed to serve young adults; namely, education, employment, military service, welfare and social services, and some aspects of religious institutions.

The young serviceman is especially caught in the trap of conflicting identity experiences. At the time in life in which he is most concerned with defining his life and assuming the appropriate roles of adulthood, he is thrust into a ready-made identity based upon mass conformity and is forced to look like every other man. The new military is highly disciplined and technically trained, resulting in a depersonalized force of men functioning as entities within a total weapons system. The basic purpose of modern militarism is to condition (to dehumanize) men to kill and destroy without conscience or remorse. The rising violence in our society is directly related to the growing number of young men who have not only been taught to use weapons but to use them without human emotion and sensitivity. Such observations cannot finally judge the necessity of a military system, but it does point clearly to the problem such a system creates for young adults.

The present hippie phenomenon is in part an act of identification, in part a rebellion against the depersonalized forces, and in part a cry asking to be identified. The bizarre dress and way of life of the hippies are symbolically saying "Look at me! Who do I say I am? Who do you say I am?" And as most of the readers know, the social response to the hippie movement has been negative, punitive, and has served only to confirm the self-image of worthlessness that they as youth have experienced already in the family, school, and other social settings dominated by adults. Many young adults are acting destructively in society today because they have never experienced a self-definition which does not say "You're a nobody!" or "You're no good!" or "You're a failure, a drag on society!"

There is yet another factor in the young adult search for a self-definition for life. Our society is presently experiencing a great deal of confusion over the sex roles and the meaning of maleness and femaleness. The young adult actually finds himself growing up in a time in which the masculine and feminine roles are becoming quite diffused. In fact, it is said that this new generation is experiencing the loss of sex, or desexualization.[8]

Apparently it is the lack of clear sexual distinction between young men and women that is so disturbing to the adult generation. The exaggerated sexuality of the John Wayne type of man and the Elizabeth Taylor type of woman is almost sculptured to young adults and seems to belong in some gallery for the display of artifacts of another era. The Beatles and Mia Farrow represent the nonsexual look which dominates young adult life today. This does not

[8] Cf. Charles Winick, *The New People* (New York: Pegasus, 1968).

mean that young adults today will not reach into the past for their fashions, as they are now doing; but they will do so more to be *camp* (fad) or to play a role than to actually reflect how they feel and exist. What is disappearing in our time are the stereotypes of strength and glamour which once characterized the masculine and feminine roles.

McLuhan's social psychology is somewhat unorthodox but does seem to be grounded in what is now taking place. In the first place, young adults are rejecting the older sexual definitions which emphasized the separateness of man and woman and the dominant and seductive roles. Such definitions were based upon disinvolvement—even in the sexual embrace—or what McLuhan calls visual identities which were "hot" or disengaging.

In the second place, young adults are adopting definitions of man and woman which are more "neuter" than distinctive. This does not mean, as some alarmists feel, that men and women are becoming any less capable as sexual beings. It does mean that the sexual roles are becoming more integrated, more expressive, and more open to involvement. As McLuhan suggests, the definition of the sexual roles are "cool" or tactile today, with greater stress on touch and participation rather than on distance. The relationships between male and female in the young adult society are based more on dialogue than on the supremacy of one of the sexes; and on the mutual sharing of feelings and desires more than on exploitation and sexual performance.[9]

[9] Marshall McLuhan and George B. Leonard, "The Future of Sex," *Look,* July 25, 1967, pp. 56-63. See also McLuhan's *Understanding Media* (New York: McGraw-Hill, 1964), pp. 120 ff.

Intimacy

The crisis which dominates the attention of the young adult until it is resolved is that of *intimacy versus isolation.* This is the need to make and maintain significant patterns of friendship and to achieve meaningful sexual relationships. Until intimacy is achieved the young adult can expect to experience various forms of isolation, incompleteness, and loneliness.

Intimacy here refers to something more than sexual intercourse. The capacity for genital relationships often precedes the capacity for mutual engagement and self-abandonment. As Erikson has pointed out, "Sexual intimacies often precede the capacity to develop a true and mutual psychosocial intimacy with another person, be it in friendship, in erotic encounters, or in joint inspiration." [10] Intimacy is first of all a psychological meeting—a dialogue that invites participation and the giving and receiving of each other. Gibson Winter has assisted us in a definition when he writes that intimacy is "the relationship in which people know one another, support one another, share their lives and identify their interests with one another." [11] It is this psychosocial experience of intimacy that transforms sexual *intimacies* into sexual *intimacy.* The integration of the erotic into the larger task of establishing personal relationships is one of the needs of young adults. Until this is done, young adults are not ready for marriage and the love and commitments which it requires.

The attempt to resolve the crises of isolation and loneli-

[10] *Identity: Youth and Crisis,* p. 135.
[11] *Love and Conflict: New Patterns in Family Life* (Garden City, N.Y.: Doubleday & Co., 1958), p. 7.

ness often takes the form of sexual activities. At least within the sexual embrace an estranged individual feels wanted, even though it is for no other reason than bodily contact. But as many young adults soon discover, the genital union is meaningless apart from the capacity for psychological union.

Friendship is a greatly overused and sentimentalized word in our vocabulary. And yet it carries the meaning which best describes the true nature of intimacy and is an essential basis for genital experiences. As the saying goes, some persons are great lovers but are lousy at friendship. Intimacy arises out of the ability to know and to share with another and to incorporate in that psychological experience the erotic and the sexual.

Although the feeling of isolation and loneliness is real for most young adults, it has possibly been overemphasized as a problem. There is evidence that once young adults are able to achieve self-definition, they are able to resolve the psychological and sexual crisis of intimacy, possibly with greater ease and with fewer breakdowns than in previous generations. The new personalism in our society has conditioned persons to move more readily and with less difficulty into relationships of depth and meaning. This is not to imply that there are not those young adults who because of fear and inhibition are unable to make intimate relationships. It does mean that the neurosis associated with genital maturity and lustful expressions may not be as severe today as in more traditional and inhibited societies. Young adults seem to be coming of age much better prepared for sexual relationships and with greater expectancy as to their meaning.

136

For those who do fail to achieve intimacy there is either severe withdrawal from relationships and from situations where engagement can be anticipated, or there is the compulsive search for pseudotypes of relationships. The latter is most often characterized by self-seeking sexual gratification or a kind of promiscuity in which persons move from one sexual partner to another without ever experiencing self-abandonment or true fusion with another. Among young adults at least—and I believe it is true of every age group—sexual problems are more symptomatic of unresolved needs than a lack of moral concern.

As Erikson has reminded us, intimacy is never really possible until the self has been fully defined. The attempt to find one's maleness or femaleness in sexual engagement is really an impossible quest. Until an individual knows himself, he is unable to abandon himself to the search to know another.[12] The establishment of oneself as a person opens the way for mutuality in all levels of relationships, including the orgastic satisfaction between man and woman. And in the search for identity the feelings of lust rise with increasing intensity, demanding expression in some satisfactory manner. It is the normal young adult who is aware of his desires and seeks to integrate them within his definition of life. The more abnormal will either pretend that lustful desires do not exist or deny their importance for life fulfillment.

Possibly one of the reasons young adults find themselves in conflict with society so much of the time is that the lustful powers are such a dominant force in their lives and

---

[12] *Identity and the Life Cycle,* pp. 124 ff.

occupy so much of their attention. Sex is feared in our culture and is generally acknowledged as only existing within the confines of marriage. Even more serious is society's inability to appreciate the creative dimensions of lust within all human relations. Lust not only gives rise to aesthetic qualities of personal existence, but also is the source of warm, tender feelings so necessary in intimate relations of friendship and love. Sex denial results in a repression of normal lust and drives underground natural explorations and attempts to find expressive forms of sexuality.

Abstraction of the lustful force from the personality pushes normal sexual concerns to the limits of the life-system and results in much sex "out there" or in the "objectification" of sex. In fact, much of the so-called sexual activity of young adults—ranging from preoccupation with sex symbols, sex pictures, and sex talk to meaningless sex acts of masturbation and depersonalized intercourse—is the manifestation of a failure to integrate lust or genitality fully within the total life-system.

Nevitt Sanford in his studies of impulse expression found that an overly strong superego or the lack of sexual integration within the personality will contribute to either impulsive sexual behavior or serious sexual inhibition and the negation of lustful powers. He writes:

> When sex is fully integrated with the ego, it can be a channel for the expression of a rich assortment of feelings and emotions. Such integration also means, of course, that sex experiences can now become a means for further development of the personality; like other important experiences, it can take place within an ex-

panding structure of integrated processes. . . . The broader the life-space, the less the chances that sex will assume overriding importance.[13]

Attempts to disassociate lust from the life-system results in a duality of sexual experiences. The young man will categorize women with whom he has relations as prostitute and good girl, sexy girl and nice girl, lustful and not lustful, and so forth. As is apparent, one kind of relation satisfies lustful needs, and another kind of relation is used to meet personal loneliness and to provide intimacy. In actuality this pattern of behavior generally contributes to anxiety, reduces the possibility of experiences which will authentically validate one's sex roles, and decreases the opportunity for sexual experiences which will lead to further integration and expansion of the life-system. In fact, according to Sullivan, the duality of sexual experiences results in serious cleavage, the loss of self-respect, and a shrinkage within the life-system.[14]

There is evidence that young adults are beginning to resist the negative approach of culture toward sex. There seems to be emerging a more positive appreciation of the power of sex and the role it can play in human relations. Young adults today do not seem as preoccupied with sex when compared with previous generations. They have certainly rejected the attempts of adult society to keep sex beyond the scope of human relations. As we pointed out in an earlier chapter, young adults today seem to be less

[13] "The Freeing and Acting Out of Impulse in Late Adolescence: Evidence from Two Cases," *The Study of Lives*, p. 31.
[14] *The Interpersonal Theory of Psychiatry*, pp. 288 ff.

promiscuous and more concerned that sexual expression takes place within a context of intimacy in which deep caring, appreciation, and mutuality are fundamental to the relationship.

We cannot close this section without pointing out that we have in our society a group of young adults who are experiencing a loss of feeling and expressiveness. These tend to be middle-class young adults who are caught up in the present pressures to achieve educationally. There is a growing number who do not seem capable of establishing meaningful interpersonal relations and who are not successfully dealing with the intimacy crises.

A significant study of these young adults has been performed by Dr. Heath. He found that many college students are more tense than other young adults, more intellectual and rational, and much more prone to repress feelings—especially those warm and tender feelings which make for significant human relationships. In short, they "play it cool" with little desire to get involved, even with the opposite sex.[15]

The growing hippie movement, the use of drugs, the compulsion to love, and the engagement in sex for sex's sake all point to excessive emotional restraint and to a fear of the expressive aspects of life. The need here is for young adults to experience the exhilaration of really living out of the depths of emotion and to experience the emotions of others. Until this happens intimacy will remain a distant goal.

[15] Douglas Heath, in informal conversation regarding unpublished research, April 15, 1967.

Productivity

The final crisis in the development of young adults is also the one that marks the beginning of adulthood. It is *productivity versus self-absorption*. This is the ability either to be productive and to make a worthwhile contribution to society or to regress inwardly upon oneself. The alternative to a productive life is an impoverished one, concerned primarily in the extension of selfish needs.

"Generativity" is Erikson's description for this phase in the life cycle. By this he means a concern for "establishing and guiding the next generation." [16] The opposite side of generativity for Erikson is stagnation and boredom. What the crisis basically involves is the drive for parenthood although Erikson acknowledges that not everyone can or should participate biologically in the procreative process. At the same time, disengagement from parenthood does not eliminate the fundamental human need to be concerned for others and to make accomplishments that will better society.

Aside from parenthood, work is the avenue in our culture for the achievement of productivity. Meaningful work is the way most persons come to the realization that they are of some worth. Unfortunately, our society values the worth of work at a time in which the opportunity for employment is rapidly decreasing, especially for the culturally impoverished. And for such persons there seem to be few creative alternatives open to them as means of experiencing worth. Even parenthood for the poor is little more than a biological event that they would prefer to

---

[16] Erikson, *Identity: Youth and Crisis*, p. 138.

141

avoid and that has little relation to the productive care needed to develop a new generation. The facts reveal that productivity is an achievement open only to the culturally affluent and that there remains a host of young adults who will never actually achieve adulthood in the full sense of its meaning.

It seems hardly necessary to raise here the problem of the undereducated and the perpetually unemployable in our society. As studies indicate, these persons are concentrated in the slums of our cities. In some neighborhoods only about 50 percent of those who graduate from high school can expect to find employment. In addition, three out of four high school dropouts are presently unemployed and are almost without hope of getting work in the immediate future. When we talk about 4 to 6 percent of our society being unemployed, we overlook the fact that most of these people are concentrated in the depressed areas of our cities. The result is an urban disease that is affecting the rest of our society in the way a small stomach cancer can infect the total organism. As early as 1961, James B. Conant predicted the urban riots that have presently thrown our society into a panic. Unfortunately, our reaction has been mainly defensive—improved riot control; and not offensive—constructive programs to assist persons to become productive and to be able to truly live as *human beings*. Conant writes,

> The building up of a mass of unemployed and frustrated Negro youth in congested areas of a city is a social phenomenon that may be compared to the piling up of inflammable material in an empty build-

142

ing of a city block. Potentialities for trouble—indeed possibilities of disaster—are surely there.[17]

Undoubtedly education is closely related to one's ability to become productive (and hence to become adult). As we have argued in previous chapters, one of our basic social problems is that we have more persons coming to young adulthood than there are jobs. This has resulted in the extension of educational requirements and the length of time that a person is expected to attend school. In spite of this the dropout rate continues to be high in almost every central city school, especially in the poverty areas. For many high school graduates as well as for school dropouts, there is no employment. They are obsolete the day they enter the labor market and have little chance of ever becoming productive in work or in any other enterprise of life. The result, as studies have indicated, is that young adults are beginning to crowd the welfare rolls in increasing numbers. In Cook County, Illinois, for example, about half of the persons on welfare are under 32.3 years of age. Even more serious, unless massive reforms are undertaken in our society, these persons will spend the rest of their lives as unproductive individuals. This is dramatized by the fact that almost 50 percent of the women on welfare do not have a literacy level adequate to participate in modern society or to interpret society to their own children.

Of course there are alternatives other than parenthood and work for the expression of productive powers. But impoverishment tends to rob an individual of the capacity to experience worth in any of the other areas. Studies indicate,

[17] *Slums and Suburbs* (New York: McGraw-Hill, 1961), p. 18.

for example, that the poor and the uneducated participate in few leisure-time programs or do anything that might expand their creative facilities. Fortunately, the newer poverty programs are designed to involve the poor and to place some responsibility upon them for formulating and directing programs for the improvement of their life situation. Such programs are making an immense contribution to the need of the poor to be productive, and have become about the only opportunity thtat many have to make a contribution and to experience worth.

Productivity is finally realized in the assumption of responsibility for humanity. Unproductivity is expressed in an irresponsible withdrawal from the issues of one's time. The immature person is one who has turned from the world in order to dwell primarily within his own selfish desires. Regardless of one's social station in life, adult maturity is achieved only as one is able to assume responsibility for the future course of human history. To fail in this will result in self-indulgence and the loss of a sense of worth. Fundamental to mature life is the capacity to make a contribution that is both needed and is of some worth to others.

Young Adult Problems

The transition from adolescence to adulthood is not without the possibility of severe problems. Within each of the developmental crises are forces that can contribute to either personal growth and health or breakdown and sickness. For most persons the move toward adulthood is made with a minimum of distress to themselves and to society.

And yet the significant number who suffer great maladjustment in the process of growing up cannot be neglected.

There are no simple causes for the problems which beset young adults. Persons bring, first of all, to young adulthood a personality that has been forming since birth and which includes varying degrees of personal resources as well as liabilities. Many problems of young adults arise because developmental crises have not been adequately resolved in childhood and adolescence.

Each individual is, secondly, a product of his times and the society in which he lives. Both the health as well as the sickness of society become manifest in the members of that society, and the young adult is especially susceptible to the social diseases that surround his growing up. The success or failure of achieving the maturity of adulthood is dependent to a large extent upon the richness of adult relationships and the resources of society. As Harvard's Robert Coles has pointed out, the growing individual can never fully be understood apart from the context of his society. The young adult is more than a product of the vicissitudes of early development; he is also a reflection of his social situation.

Because of the problems of growing up and becoming adult, some young adults fall to the temptation to regress to a permanent state of adolescence. In this way they can avoid the demands of an adult life as well as the problems and responsibilities which it brings. They are seldom problems to society, but they also are rarely able to make any significant contribution to it. Sometimes these individuals will become overly dependent on young adult clubs, church groups, or other protective situations where they can hide from life and not have to face the demands of adult responsibility.

There are other young adults who are psychologically and socially alienated and who are prone to lash out against society and its institutions. Often their problems will so overwhelm them that they will attempt to express their fears and frustrations in extremely antisocial behavior, including acts of destruction and violence.

Some of the problems which seem to be particularly characteristic of the transition from adolescence to adulthood are:

1. Poor Mental Health. Some young adults not only suffer from extreme anxiety and guilt but are particularly susceptible to mental illness. Schizophrenia and various forms of psychological depression are prominent among young adults. In fact, about 75 percent of persons suffering from schizophrenia are of young adult age.

2. Divorce. About one half of all divorces involve persons under twenty-nine years of age with most of them occurring during the first three to five years of marriage. As is well known, divorce is only one of the symptoms of the strain and stress of early marriage, and there is evidence that many young adults do not make the adjustments of the husband and wife relationship without suffering much pain and unhappiness.

3. Suicide. The suicide rate among young adults has been increasing rapidly during the last decade. About one thousand college students take their lives each year, another nine thousand make an attempt, and ninety thousand more threaten suicide.

4. College Dropout. A growing number of students

are giving up and dropping out of college (and the rate of noncollege young adults who drop out of society has also been growing). Approximately 60 percent of any freshman class either leave college, or are dropped, because of inability to meet the demands of the educational situation. Studies show that many who cannot make it through college are suffering from emotional stress, resulting from the demands of young adult development.

5. *Sexual Problems.* As we have observed earlier, sex is one of the major avenues for acting out some of the deeper crises of growing up. Illegitimacy among young adults is pronounced, especially among the minorities and the other socially dispossessed. Homosexuality has also increased, and is generally considered a problem most characteristic of young adults.

6. *Crime.* Persons under thirty years of age make up the rising prison population. Especially in the area of hard core crimes—murder, rape, armed robbery—the young adult arrest rate is higher than any other age group.

7. *Anomie.* A catchall problem which describes the general disorganization of many young adults, including their inability to make attachment, their discontinuity with society, their tendency toward rulelessness. The use of drugs among some young adults is more related to this general psychological state than to any other reason.

The evidence seems clear that with all of the potentialities of a technological age growing up has became more complex and has increased the possibility of individuals experiencing personal and social breakdown. For all too many young adults, becoming adult does not seem like a worthwhile venture in a society which does not offer any goals that for them are attainable. They are caught in the web of social deterioration resulting from urbanization and technology. Possibly the power structures of our society could be forgiven for the enormous loss and waste of its young adult generation if the problems were unsolvable. But the truth of the matter is that a nation such as ours has both the resources and the knowhow to insure that a larger number of its youth can successfully move into adulthood and become equipped to make a contribution to the future of their nation.

Hanging over the problems of young adults is an older ideology which believes that every individual must be a self-made man and, if he fails in that, then the problem is one of personal morality and individual worth and not one of social reform. Rather than providing the means by which each person may more realistically realize his human life, our society tends to respond to these personal failures and social deviations with increased attempts to punish and to control.

6
The Way of the Future

There is greater significance in the young adult situation than the fact that this age group is in our society in great numbers and is able to make its presence felt in impressive ways. It is the task of theology to ask what this significance is.

Theology can be broadly defined as man thinking about God. The mode in which thinking takes place varies from culture to culture and from one historical era to another. The theologian may begin his thinking by reflecting upon scripture, church doctrines, or the human situation. It is this latter concern—the systematic reflection upon man before God in the present sociocultural situation—that characterizes much contemporary theology, including the task of this particular chapter.

Auguste Comte understood sociology to be secularized theology. He felt that you could not basically separate the theological task from the sociological. It is the attempt to once again relate theology to sociology and the other human sciences that has given rise to the new social theology. Anthropology, psychology, and sociology serve theology in its attempt to understand what God is presently doing and saying through the events of history. It is in the world and in the midst of the human situation that theology must search today for understanding and ultimate meaning. The human sciences, when read theologically, push us beyond the descriptive (what is?) to an understanding of what is happening (what it means?).

Gibson Winter has suggested that biblical and systematic theologians reflect theologically on God before man, while the social and empirical theologians reflect theologically on man before God. It is this way of considering theology that Peter Berger had in mind when he characterized Bonhoeffer's worldly theology as the work of discerning the presence of Christ in the empirical, historical, and the social reality of the world.

Much of our study of the young adult situation thus far has been empirical; that is, an attempt to accurately describe what is taking place. We wish in this chapter now to turn to some reflections as to what it means.

A Prophetic Generation

There is, in the first place, a note of the prophetic within this new generation of young adults. In their protests and demonstrations as well as in their general style of life young adults are trying to tell us something. They are trying to say that there are some things basically wrong with life in our times, and they are pointing out the pitfalls as well as the possibilities for life in the future.

It is probably not an overstatement to suggest that young adults have largely been responsible for the recovery of the prophetic voice. The function of prophecy is to bring judgment upon the complacent and to visualize both the evils as well as the promises inherent in the social situation. In doing these things, prophets seldom rely upon the written or spoken word. The Old Testament prophets were action oriented, "demonstrators" who departed from established customs and norms in order to dramatize the extent to which injustices had taken over the life of a group of people. They were the dissenters, the eccentrics, the social dropouts, and the activists. Using extreme forms of personal conduct, these Old Testament prophets confronted directly the people of power—including the ruling class—and forced a recognition of the pressing issues of society. Prophecy always included promises of dire consequences if reforms were not undertaken.

Rarely, if ever, in human history has a nation been made so sensitive to its social problems as has this nation in the 1960's. This is largely due to the actions of young adults who in one way or another have shaken every institution and social structure in the American society. The confrontations between young adults and the power groups of adult society have resulted in a visualizing of the injustices in our way of life and a dramatization of how our society has refused to allow all men the freedom and dignity that human life presupposes. Whatever else they are saying, young adults have made it clear that middle-class goals and the liberal ideology are no longer relevant to a technological age and a multiracial society. Young adults have been able to show how deeply antidemocratic values have penetrated the fiber of the American way of life. They have also been effective in forcing out into the open the contradictions between what adults say they believe and what they actually practice.

Probably more than any other one thing young adults have brought forth a sign that the old order is ending and a new one is beginning. With the urgency and impatience of youth they have insisted that life must get with the new times. Although their actions have not always been mature or represented responsible judgments, they have been sensitive to human needs and have been agitators for social change and reform. More than any other group of people in society the new generation of young adults has provided the impetus for a new kind of society.

Historians later will undobutedly acknowledge that it was the prophetic zeal of young adults that created what will be known as the human revolution of the 1960's. First came the sit-ins in the south and later the civil rights demonstrations in both south and north. They caused the nation to become slowly aware of how extensively segregation, both real and *de facto*, did exist in this country and how widespread was the prejudice existing within middle-class society.

Next came the hippie movement, made up primarily of young adults who had become discouraged with the prospects of real social reforms in their time and who had decided that a new society would come about only as people took seriously the power of love in interpersonal relationships. In protest against the growing depersonaliza-

152

tion of society and the increasing red tape associated with modern bureaucracy, these young adults dropped out of society to form communes based upon appreciation for the personal, the free expression of love, and the primacy of experience. They made apparent how intolerant society was of divergent ways of life and how uniform human experience had become in this country.

The peace demonstrators were the third prophetic movement of young adults. It was almost entirely due to the efforts of young adults that the war in Vietnam became the focus of national debate. After repeated attempts to be heard by the power structures young adults in the tradition of prophecy resorted to extreme measures—the disruption of military recruitment, the burning of draft cards, and unlawful marches—in order to awaken the conscience of the nation. The success of this movement is attested by the way the war has been resisted by all age groups and has become a major political issue. The power of this young adult generation was fully realized when it transformed the token presidential campaign of Eugene McCarthy into a serious challenge to the incumbent and other potential candidates.

There is probably no institution in our society that is any more paternalistic and authoritarian than higher education. Still another movement of young adults has been the "university take-overs," the demand for a larger role by students in the policies of the colleges and universities and for extensive reforms in higher education. The protests of the students became extremely militant and at times bordered upon anarchy, but the nation was shocked into awareness of how insensitive higher education had been to the pressing needs of the communities in which colleges and universities were located and how far the schools had departed from liberal and humanitarian education in order to serve the needs of business and military agencies.

All of this serves to point up the truth that young adults in this society have become a prophetic force. In theological language young adults have discerned the action of God and have joined in his work of humanizing the life of men. They have responded to the call to become catalysts for a society that had become preoccupied with its affluence and complacent to the dispossessed who had become hidden in the bureaucracy of human efficiency.

In a very penetrating interpretation of the young adult revolution the famed sociologist Daniel P. Moynihan has suggested that there is something Christian about this new generation. Like the Christians of second-century Rome, they are bad citizens—intolerant, disobedient toward civil authority, completely secular, odd in their dress and habits, avoiding service in the military, caring more for the outcast than the respectable, and seditious and revolutionary in character. Moynihan goes on to say that there are young adults who have become modern heretics (they reject the ideology that no one else will dare question) who have spoken to the "rational, tolerant, reasonable society of the present with the same irrationality, intolerance, and unreasonableness, but possibly also the same truth with which the absurd Christians spoke to imperial Rome." [1]

[1] Daniel P. Moynihan, "Nirvana Now," *The American Scholar,* Autumn, 1967, p. 542.

Ethical Man

One of the most significant theological issues posed by the new young adult generation is the question of the ethical life. As we have already pointed out, the popular concept that young adults are flagrantly rejecting the morality of the adult society and are amoral or even immoral in their ethical style is not borne out by empirical research. If anything, young adults are probably more ethically alert and sensitive than the adult generation as a whole. What young adults are telling us is that a new ethical man is emerging.

The issue that has become paramount for this generation is the relationship between freedom and structure. Within the young adult generation (as well as the adult society) are those whose concern for freedom borders upon anarchy. They believe that *all* of the present structures and institutions of society are totally corrupt and that the only alternative is to completely disregard them. We see within the young adult situation those whose major concern is to do what they please, regardless of the welfare of others or the long-range consequences of their actions upon the future course of history. Personal urges and desires become the bases out of which ethical decisions are made.

The movie *Alfie* offers one of the best examples of a nonconforming young adult. Moving from girl to girl in order to satisfy his sexual and egotistical needs, Alfie refuses to get seriously involved in any question which transcends him as a person. His own search for pleasure and personal satisfaction dominates his life, and when he contributes to the destruction of other individuals, he shrugs it off as no concern of his.

This results in a totalitarian form of freedom. As sociologist Leonard Blumberg points out, some young adults are actually demanding the removal of all controls and the imposition of their brand of freedom upon all of society. This new kind of moralism would in final reality become every bit as redundant as the old moralism. To imperialize in absolute categories the values of freedom and personal expression is just as legalistic as were the older categories of law and moral norms.

On the other side are those who attempt to describe the ethical man completely in terms of traditional moral structures. Here the ethical life is defined primarily in normative patterns of behavior and prescribed rules to be applied to every ethical situation. Answers formulated in another era are expected to be as applicable to new ethical situations as they were in the older ones. Traditional man places greater worth upon structures than upon the needs of individuals and the requirements of a changing society. Law is basic to the ethical life and reflects the need to maintain order as well as to maintain the stability of institutions and structures of society. Morality is best insured by the law, and those who deviate should be punished in order to insure goodness and discourage evil. Deviation from the norm or the patterns of the majority is looked upon as wrong and intolerable.

Graham Greene's novel *A Burnt-Out Case* is a story of how a traditional and legalistic Christian destroys a good but irreligious man. Querry, a world famous architect and a noted collector of women, seeks to escape from life by going to a Catholic leper colony in the Congo. There he performs acts of heroism and, in spite of his rejection of tradition and his adulterous activities, is able to respond with great sensitivity to human misery. He is seen by almost everyone as another Schweitzer and a saint.

In the same colony is a Catholic layman who is more than proud of his religious dedication and loyalty to traditional Christianity. Greene describes him as the kind of man who can say all of the right words and perform the proper religious acts, but who is also empty in the presence of human needs. Like many traditionalists, he formally meets all the requirements of a good life, but always in abstraction, oblivious to the needs of those around him. Greene describes him as being "like a wall so plastered over with church announcements that you couldn't even see the brick work behind." In the end his suspicious superspirituality destroys the architect.

The traditional man bases the ethical life upon structures, including law, rules, and normative codes, and fails to understand that prescribed answers do not always fit the needs of modern man or the changing demands that a technological age creates.

It seems to me that a third alternative for the ethical life is emerging in this generation. This might be characterized as the responsible man or the ethical life that is firmly rooted in the present but is open to the insights and guidelines arising from the past. To be responsible in the complex issues of a new society is to find the most appropriate ways to love in order that the personal dignity of individuals as well as the order of a community can be actualized. The responsible man is an evaluating, deciding, and acting man. He responds to the needs and issues of humanity in the most appropriate manner possible. In the responsible man there is the possibility for a realistic, structured freedom.

As we indicated earlier, there is evidence that young adults are in the process of formulating a new ethic, based largely upon the behavioral sciences, which can be described as a humanistic ethic. What has emerged is a worldly ethic based uncritically upon a rejection of religion in general and Christianity in particular. The humanistic ethic actually arises out of Christianity, and the tragedy is that most young adults have never had an adequate understanding of the tradition which they think they are rejecting. In embracing a humanistic ethic they are to a certain extent embracing the Christian doctrine of incarnation and the belief that a radical humanism was the subject of God's action. By rejecting Christianity they fail to enjoy the roots of their ethical system, and they do not have the resources to make corrections in faulty thinking. Even the hippies in their folk ethic have become realistic enough to realize that sin is a potent force in the human experience, and as a result they have been forced to seek out some sort of religious orientation in order to have a perspective for ethical judgments.

If young adults would take a new look at Christianity and its resources for an ethical life, they would find that central to that tradition is human love. Love is Christianity's major contribution to the new age and to the new ethical demands upon man. The central act of being human for the Christian is the act of love directed toward other men.

The new ethical man will not cut himself off from tradition or turn to structures as ends in themselves. Neither will he seek freedom for himself at the expense of other people. He will allow tradition to enrich the present and will seek to find those structures which will order human life and provide the maximum freedom for all men.

Our model for a responsible humanity is Jesus. In him we find a consensus between personal freedom and social structures. In Jesus we have a vision of what it means to be truly human. It is to be liberated and free, but disciplined; it is to be fearless in the presence of uncertainties; it is to have the ability to improvise in the face of new situations; and it is to be in love with life and to have concern for the whole community of men. In short to be ethical is to be human.

A Theology of Change

A third thing that young adults seem to be saying is that we must come to live with the continuous prospect of change and to appreciate the dynamic nature of the modern world. To resist change and to turn from the future is sin. As Robert Oppenheimer has declared, "To assail change that has unmoored us from the past is futile, and in a deep sense, I think, it is wicked. We need to recognize the change and learn what resources we have." In this young adult generation we may come to understand what Christianity has long believed: the gospel calls us to leave the past behind and to move with hope and confidence into the future. Eschatology is the doctrine that is concerned with the Christian hope for the future. To be a Christian is to believe in change and the promises that it brings.

159

A mood that is deeply ingrained in our society is pessimism. One can understand why such negativism exists within the slums of the city and the ranks of the unemployed. But the real thrust of pessimism arises from those who fear the future and whose security is threatened by change. And it is these persons, mostly the affluent, who find solace in the past. To a large extent these are the persons who are adherents to the Christian faith and are members of the churches. It has been a part of the religious tradition in American society to glorify the past and to believe that what once was is better than what is to be.

In the midst of a changing social scene the temptation is to attach oneself with religious zeal to the more recent past. As a result we have in our society those persons who are inclined to become satisfied with life as it is and who will resist change of any kind. They are the persons McLuhan describes as moving backward into the future. They are the followers of Billy Graham, the members of Campus Crusade, and the persons who make up the other conservative groups which promote the "old-time religion" and the "good old days." For them the gospel never changes, and the essence of the Christian life is to reduplicate the life of earlier Christians.

It is not possible within the scope of this study to fully formulate a theology of change. That such a theology is needed is very much apparent in the preoccupation that young adults have with change as well as with the future. All that can be done at this point is to include some brief reflections as to the direction such a theology might take.

1. The belief in change and in the future does not rest in the naïve optimism that life is going to get better

all the time. As any observer will recognize, change does not necessarily result in a better quality of human life. In fact, all change is ambiguous, resulting always in both new problems as well as new opportunities. As Thomas W. Ogletree points out, Christian hope avoids the pitfalls of optimism and despair. In commenting upon the theology of hope of Jürgen Moltmann, Ogletree writes:

> Christian hope does not tempt man presumptuously to overestimate his capacities for reshaping his world. It enables him to face frankly the depth and intensity of problems which normally thwart any meaningful changes in the order of life. At the same time, Christian hope does not permit man to submit to the destructive limits of the existing situation. It sets before him the promise of a genuinely new reality which contradicts that situation, which opens up possibilities that bring its negativities to nought.[2]

2. As we have already observed, young adults seem to have little sense of history, and therefore they have little understanding of the significance of change. Now history refers to more than the past, although the past is essential to an appreciation of the present as well as to the forecasting of the future. History is also concerned with present actions, events, and changes. For the Christian, history is significant for two reasons. First, it is within history that truth is comprehended. The Word which was in Christ was not a static word to be understood only once in history. As Karl Barth reminds us, the Word also becomes time. It

[2] "Reflection on a Theology of Hope," *Christian Advocate*, April 4, 1968, p. 7.

becomes history, and it is within the events of change that Jesus Christ comes again and again to man.

Second, God as creator and actor is within history. Creation is a continuous process, and God is ever acting in the events of change. The Christian faith believes that God is speaking to man through the events of history. It is the responsibility of the Christian to discern what God is doing in the world and to join in his work. Change is the process by which man shares in the ongoing work of creation and the full realization of the God who lives in the affairs of men.

3. An understanding of change makes possible new and fresh ways to talk about God and provides new symbols in which to express the ultimate meaning by which man is to live. As Harvey Cox has argued, the present revolutions of urban society are providing us with new ways of conceptualizing our faith in order that the Word might once again be delivered fresh. The symbols of the city and the language of politics provide one way to keep theology dynamic and relevant to the experiences of man.[3]

As we reexamine the Christian basis for a theology of change, it becomes increasingly clear that an age of change is a *time for Christians*. With young adults we are discovering that change is not an occasion for fear but an opportunity to assume responsibility for the future.

Transcendence

A fourth theological observation has to do with the extent that young adults reflect the loss of transcendence

---

[3] *The Secular City*, chap. 5.

throughout society. At the same time there is among some young adults a minor trend toward recovering a sense of transcendence.

The extent to which our society has lost a sense of transcendence is reflected in how far most of us go in order to avoid the word God—except possibly in connection with patriotic ceremonies. As one young adult hippie put it, "My parents are embarrassed to say 'God,' but we are not. I can say 'God' and mean that life is larger than me, or even me and my lover."

Also the "cult of the present" that cuts across part of our society reflects how limited modern men are in their perspective. The tragedy is that the attempts to seek the modern as an end generally disintegrate into a vague nothingness, resulting in a decay of man and the shrinking of his ability to experience himself as well as others.

The quest for the Spirit on the part of some young adults suggest that they are coming to recognize that life has little significance unless an individual is able to get beyond himself. The recovery of the transcendence will possibly not come in traditional concepts of the supernatural and its emphasis upon union with a God that lies beyond the scope of human experiences. There is urgent need to listen to the young adults who are experimenting with meditation and mind expansion. And it is essential that theology be open to whatever truth is in the present utilization of drugs as a means toward experiencing the transcendence. Even such persons as McLuhan seem to be helping us to get above the immediate situation and to probe and discover what is around us in the ordinary experiences of life.

Transcendence has always meant to get beyond the immediate and to experience a connection with the larger dimensions of life. As we have seen in the first chapter, we are living in an age that is getting along without God as a problem solver. But even in such a cultural situation man needs a larger perspective and a greater sense of depth than he can provide through his own resources. He needs an expansion of his own experiences and a sense of belonging to a unity of experiences that transcend both time and history. Possibly this is what theology calls the "holy" or the "sacred." In any case theology of transcendence for the secular man is waiting to be fully formulated. But through young adults we are beginning to realize that it is essential to human existence in the future electropolis.

As we move into the future with all of its possibilities as well as pitfalls, a new kind of life will be required. This life is possibly emerging in the new young adult generation. They are the wave of the future and are providing us with a glimpse of a new era. I believe that the future belongs to man and that we are on the verge of a new humanism. Such a humanism will deliver man from his narrow provincialism into a new sense of community and a greater willingness to share life with others. The future will not be free of conflict. There will remain also the tremendous possibility that the human race may totally destroy itself. But hopefully, in the recovery of a greater sense of the human, man will learn to resolve his conflicts at the conference table and not by war.

As we move toward the future, we will learn to live with greater diversity and a greater openness to the new. And what is even more essential, man will find that as he breaks the shackles of traditionalism the future will help him discover anew the God of his fathers.

The new world will require a new man. Through young adults we are experiencing a prototype of what will be required of this new man as he lives in a highly complex technological society.

1. He will have to live in an urban technology that will be completely secular. It is in such a culture that man will celebrate the joys of his humanness.

2. He will need to learn to live in an open-ended civilization with his uncertainty and with only provisional answers as a resource.

3. He will find life increasingly diversified, which means that he will have to appreciate those who are different from himself and at the same time keep his own integrity and maintain his own personal identity.

4. In order that the rapid changes of history do not break him down, he will need a larger perspective on history, using his resources of faith and the ability to transcend the immediate in order to grasp larger blocks of experiences and human meanings.

5. He will need to learn to live on the boundary situations between rigid alternatives (in the grey areas of life rather than the black and white).

6. Life will require dreamers and visionaries able to see the possibilities in change and to take responsibility for shaping their society. They will need to be innovators.

It is in a world coming of age that man may possibly find himself once again and in the process find that the God who has forsaken us is actually the God who is with us.

Index

Suicide, 146
Sullivan, Harry Stack, 97, 99, 118, 119, 120, 131, 139
Summer, William G., 89
Supernaturalism, 13, 83, 84
  decline of, 94
  psychological, 84
Symonds, Percival M., 127

Technology, 14, 15, 27, 28, 29-31, 57, 68
Theological conceptualizing, 162
Theology, 149
  of change, 159-61
  of culture, 6
  empirical, 150
  and ethics, 157
  and human sciences, 150
  secular, 73, 82, 83, 149
  social, 13
  supernaturalism, 13, 83, 84
  worldly, 150
Totalitarian, 156
Tradition, 16, 24, 46
  new humanitarian, 69
  religious, 86
Transcendentalism, 76
Transitional age, 97
Trent, James W., 81
Trow, Martin, 59

Universities, 25
Urban, 27, 165
  life, 23, 98
  man, 22
  opportunities, 21
  problems, 21
  riots, 142

Urban—*cont'd*
  world, 20, 25
Urbanization, 16, 20, 23, 30, 148

Values
  adult, 38
  and beliefs, 37, 42
  culture, 45
  human, 18, 38, 88
  humanistic, 44, 56, 67, 68, 88
  middle-class, 19, 38, 44, 46, 56, 67, 107
  parental, 65
  private, 37
  young adult, 37, 38, 45
Victorianism, 89
Vocation, 129

Watts, William A., 80, 81
White, R. H., 97
White, Winston, 52
Whittaker, David, 80, 81
Winick, Charles, 133
Winograd, Barry, 90
Winter, Gibson, 16, 135, 150
Work, 126, 141, 143

Young adult
  age specialization, 24
  configuration model of development, 110-21
  development, 110-21
  developmental tasks, 106-8
  ethical life, 155, 156
  expectations, 25, 26
  generation, 11, 12, 27, 28, 36, 39, 148, 150, 164
  homogeneity, 55
  influence of, 17